Servants' Hall

Also by Margaret Powell

Below Stairs: The Classic Kitchen Maid's Memoir That Inspired
"Upstairs, Downstairs" and "Downton Abbey"

Margaret Powell's Cookery Book: 500 Upstairs Recipes from
Everyone's Favorite Downstairs *Kitchen Maid and Cook*

Servants' Hall

A Real Life *Upstairs, Downstairs* Romance

Margaret Powell

St. Martin's Griffin
New York

www.stmartins.com

The Library of Congress Cataloging-in-Publication data is available upon request.

ISBN 978-1-250-04345-0 (trade paperback)
ISBN 978-1-250-02928-7 (e-book)

St. Martin's Griffin books may be purchased for educational, business, or promotional use. For information on bulk purchases, please contact Macmillan Corporate and Premium Sales Department at 1-800-221-7945, extension 5442, or write specialmarkets@macmillan.com.

Previously published in London by Michael Joseph

First St. Martin's Griffin Edition: January 2014

10 9 8 7 6 5 4 3 2

To my long-ago, but not forgotten, friends, the servants
who helped to banish 'basement blues'

Author's note

The story of Rose is a true one but other names
and places have been slightly changed.

1

In 1922, when at the age of fifteen I entered domestic service – after two years as a 'daily' – servants were considered less than dusty by those who employed them; and ignorant, even positively 'not all there' by that section of the working class, male and female alike, who wouldn't have been seen alive, or dead, as a servant 'below stairs'.

Regardless of their poor wages and often poverty-stricken home lives, shop girls were the romantic dreamers. Didn't they all day long handle delicate fabrics, perfumes and jewelry? Didn't they serve titled ladies and debutantes; and just serve them, not wait on them hand and foot as domestic servants did? Furthermore, shop girls had the opportunity to meet dashing and obviously wealthy young men, who were not averse to a little dalliance with a pretty girl behind the counter. Small wonder that many a girl had visions of marrying one of those desirable and delectable prizes.

But servant girls too had their dreams. We found them in the pages of *Peg's Paper* and *The Crimson Circle* where the heroines, without surrendering a fraction of their innocence and virginity, eventually succeeded in capturing the love – and money – of the handsome hero. We found romance, excitement and vicarious sexual emotion in the cinema, swooning over such cardboard lovers as Rudolph

Valentino or Ramon Navarro. Though, as I used to say to my friend Gladys, it couldn't be all honey being courted by one of those sheik types. When he held you in a passionate embrace, you wouldn't know for sure whether he really cared or was just getting in a bit of practice for his next film. Gladys reckoned that she'd take a chance on it, for at least they didn't start off by trying to feel a girl in all the wrong places – as the fellows one met at a dance did.

At the films, we too, for a while, could be as sexy as a Clara Bow, or as slinkily seductive as a Pola Negri. But one place where we never at any time looked for romance was above stairs. Although living in the same house, coming into contact in bedrooms, drawing-rooms and kitchen, those above stairs were, to servants, a world apart. None of us dreamed, or thought the prospect even remotely possible, of entering their life, of being one of them. Their style, their money and perhaps even their morals, were totally alien to the way of life below stairs. So, no matter if the sons or nephews occasionally visited the kitchen and servants' hall on some specious excuse, we knew well enough they were merely amusing themselves by slumming. And yet, during my years in service, one girl did manage to change her status from downstairs to upstairs by marrying the son of the house; much to the Madam's dismay and the Master's fury. I must admit that Rosalie, the parlourmaid, was an exceptionally pretty girl – though a bit slow in the uptake. She had a lovely creamy skin, the bluest of eyes, and thick golden hair that waved naturally. I'd have thought that with those natural advantages, she could have got a better job than being a parlourmaid. But Rosalie's mother was a strict, church-going disciplinarian, the embodiment of respectability. So what better job for her daughter than domestic service; that was eminently respectable.

All this occurred over fifty years ago. There are only two of us left now; Mary the under-housemaid, and me. I am therefore able to write about a unique event and the life of the household.

2

I was eighteen when I decided that I was fed up with being a kitchenmaid; fed up with having to gauge the disposition of the cook and cater to her whims and fancies; fed up with having to wait on the other servants. I reckoned I'd learnt enough about cooking to become a good plain cook. So I decided to give a month's notice and then to go home for a couple of weeks – I'd saved enough money to pay my mother for my keep – while I looked around for another job and a new status.

One needed a short interval between leaving the old job and entering the basement of a new one, because working out a month's notice was purgatory. The cook was invariably extremely irritated because you wanted to get away from her, and she'd also have to start training another girl. Yet, however awful she was, it would have been very unwise to answer rudely because she might tell Madam that you weren't a good kitchenmaid, and then, if Madam didn't give you a good reference, you'd no hope of getting a decent job.

I'd always kept in contact with Mary, the under-housemaid from my first job below stairs, so I wrote to let her know that I contemplated taking a job as a cook. Mary was still an under-housemaid, working now in a large country house near Southampton. I'd been home only two days when she came to see me, principally with the object of persuading me to become a temporary kitchenmaid. In a week's time they would be in urgent need of one.

'It's ever such a nice place, Margaret. Madam, Mrs Wardham, is a lovely lady to work for, so considerate. *He*'s a bit of a swine, but then you'd never see him, he never goes down to the basement except once in a while to inspect the wine cellar. And it's only for a month or two, until the cook's niece can come as a kitchenmaid. There's a between-maid so you'd get help in the kitchen; and Mrs Buller, the cook, though she's a bit churchy, she's easy to get on with.'

'Don't make me laugh, Mary. You're always telling me that people *you* don't have to work under are easy to get on with. Yet when I told you that I quite liked Alice, the upper housemaid where we were at Mrs Clydesdale, you went up in the air and said she was an old witch. Still, you were right about the cook there; Mrs McIlroy was quite nice.'

'There you are then, Margaret. She's married now too.'

'Married? Never! Not Mrs McIlroy. Why, she was fifty at least. Who would marry her?'

'You remember the butler, Mr. Wade? He got the sack for going out in one of the reverend's suits and coming home as drunk as a lord. Mrs McIlroy married him about a month ago. I expect she thought, any port in a storm. Anyway, he's got a good job as a hall porter in a posh hotel. Ah! that was a night, wasn't it, when he got the sack; made a lovely bit of excitement for us. D'you remember he came rolling in about ten o'clock, went into his bedroom and came out with a sheet draped round him like a surplice. Then, waving a whisky bottle in one hand and a Bible in the other, he shouted to us goggle-eyed servants, "Down on your knees, sinners" – like we had to at prayers every morning with that old hypocrite the reverend giving us sermons on counting our blessings. Then Mr Wade said:

Dearly beloved brethren, isn't it a sin,
to eat new potatoes and throw away the skin.
Though the skins feed the pigs and the pigs feed us,
Dearly beloved brethren, eat them you must.

'Ah! Wasn't Mr Wade the one for making up rhymes at the drop of a hat.'

'Yes, but worse than that, Mary, was when he went on imitating the reverend's voice, saying, "Here endeth the first lesson", and then to our horror – because we could see the reverend on the basement stairs – adding, "I'm as drunk as I can be, all on the reverend's fine whisky. What a stingy old man is he".'

We had almost burst trying to suppress our laughter while the reverend was there – for we hadn't wanted to follow Mr Wade into the wilderness. But up in our bedroom we'd giggled like mad over the thunder-struck expression on the reverend's face; such an outrageous event had never been known in the reverend's house. That a servant should get drunk and utter blasphemous words! It was worth a month's wages, £2, to have been a spectator.

These reminiscences didn't deflect Mary from the purpose of her visit. When I asked why couldn't they manage in the Wardham house with just the between-maid if it was only for one month, she said that Mrs Buller needed somebody who could cook for the servants and make sauces because, as Madam was giving her niece a London Season, there was a lot of entertaining going on in the house. I was about to protest that obviously there must be a lot of work, when Mary hastened to explain that Madam didn't expect the servants to do all the extra work for nothing. She thanked them all, and often gave them extra money. To listen to Mary the place sounded like a domestic's dream of heaven.

'Yes, Mary, that's all very well,' I said, 'but I was just about to write after this job advertised in the *Morning Post:* GOOD PLAIN COOK REQUIRED. £40 PER ANNUM. OWN BEDROOM. USUAL FREE TIME AND ONE WHOLE DAY OFF PER MONTH. It's in Belgravia.'

'For the last year we've had one whole day off a month, and we're allowed to stay out until eleven o'clock on that night. As for wages, I know the kitchenmaid gets £30 a year; that's not bad, is it?'

With such inducements offered me I couldn't turn it down. So, some days later, and carrying only a suitcase as I wasn't staying long, I travelled by train to Southampton and then got on a bus to this remote country residence. I suppose it wasn't all that remote, really, but to me, used to crowds of people and shops, the bus seemed to be going into the back of beyond. I felt considerably dismayed when at last, after more than an hour's ride, I was set down at the gates of a very long drive. What on earth would I do with my free time in this place, with not a sign of habitation, people, shops and cinemas? The rain was pouring down, and owing to the tall trees which almost met overhead the broad drive looked dark and uninviting. I trudged along, with rain dripping through the trees onto me, until I came to an arrow pointing to Tradesmen's Entrance – I was experienced enough to know that the front door wasn't for me.

I always found it an ordeal meeting the other servants because, unlike shop and factory workers who spent only a number of specified hours together, in domestic service we were confined in a limited space from early morning until late at night. We needed to keep on good terms with one another; it was too embarrassing otherwise.

Mary was getting the servants' tea so I sat in the servants' hall and met the others. There was the cook, Mr Hall the butler, Annie the upper-housemaid, Doris the tweeny, and Rosalie the parlourmaid – being trained by the butler. Later on I met the valet and ladies' maid. The servants' hall was a considerable improvement on my last one. Floral wallpaper, a few pictures and ornaments, and comfortable rugs on the linoleum certainly made it look like a sitting-room and not the waiting-room of some institution. I couldn't help staring at Rose – as she was called there – she was so pretty. Even the black afternoon uniform and white cap couldn't detract from her good looks. In comparison with Rose, whose features looked as though they were sculptured, the rest of us might have been moulded from putty. However, some consolation was to be found in contemplating the poor tweeny, Doris; she not only had lank mousey hair, but a squint too. I found out later on that she came from an orphanage, and she had one of the kindest of dispositions. Unfortunately, at the village hops, lank mousey hair and a squint were great disadvantages; young men just weren't interested in the nice disposition.

The kitchen was the usual very large room with flag-stones covered with strips of brown coconut matting. The usual huge dresser took up one wall, and the equally huge kitchen range almost all the other. There was, too, a small gas stove on which Mrs Buller cooked the breakfast and kept the dishes hot until needed. She also baked simply wonderful soufflés in it although the oven had no Regulo; one had to use judgement and a lot of commonsense. Nowadays, with all the automatic kitchen equipment, judgement and commonsense are of little use. What one needs to be now is a qualified engineer, electrician and gas-fitter so that when the labour-saving devices break down, as they frequently do, one doesn't go mad with irritation waiting for the experts to call.

After tea, Mary and Rose took me up to the bedroom that I was to share with them – Doris had a little boxroom. Although there were three beds, we weren't cramped and we each had a washstand. Also, wonder of wonders, there was a bathroom for the servants which we could use any day we liked – after first enquiring whether the upper servants would be using it. I said to Mary and Rose how nice it would be when we got to be upper servants, then we'd have all the privileges. Mary, who was a year older than me, said she didn't intend to be in service long enough to become an upper-housemaid. When her merchant navy boyfriend came home from this voyage they were going to be married.

'When will that be?' Rose enquired.

'Oh, not for another year yet, it's a two-year voyage.'

'Oh, Mary, fancy having a boyfriend that you can't see for two years. What ever do you do when you want to go to dances, and you engaged and all.'

'Well, silly, I don't tell boys. Besides, I'm not really engaged, it's just an understanding. Sid knows that I go to dances, he don't expect me not to have any fun while he's away. He trusts me.'

I couldn't help feeling that he must be a singularly trustful young man; because if one was lucky enough to get a partner in a dance hall he invariably became somewhat amorous. The type of dances encouraged that feeling, for dancing waltzes and foxtrots one was held in close embrace. Even so, we were all encased in heavily-boned corsets, held so rigid it was like wearing armour, and a young man wasn't exactly clasping a mass of palpitating flesh. But if you didn't respond at all to his advances, then, unless you were a marvellous dancer, that would be the one and only time he'd ask you to dance and you would find yourself joining the other wallflowers. A girl as pretty as Rose, though, whether or not she was a good dancer, would never lack for a partner.

On her bedside table there was a picture of a young man. Rose said that her mother wanted her to marry him, he earned good money working in a mill in Manchester – where Rose lived. 'Are you going to?' I asked, and Rose said that she supposed she would some day, her mum liked this Len.

'You're not going to have him just because your mum likes him, are you? Besides,' I added, 'his ears stick out like jug handles, he'll never be able to wear a bowler hat.'

Mary started to laugh as she told us she had once a boyfriend with large floppy ears and every time he got a bit passionate not only did he breathe heavily, but his ears waggled like deflated balloons; it was a good warning that he was about to get inflated elsewhere. Rose screeched, 'Oh, Mary, you are awful.'

By this time I'd changed into my uniform and was all ready for work downstairs. Mary had already told me that the family consisted of Mr and Mrs Wardham, an unmarried daughter of about thirty-five, an eighteen-year-old niece, and a son, about thirty, who'd only recently returned home after three years farming in Rhodesia. According to Mr Hall, the butler, the son had come back because he couldn't make a go of it out there. This had greatly incensed his father who'd put up the money for the project.

3

As I'd never worked in a house with a between-maid, I wondered just what our spheres of activity were. Mrs Buller told me that Doris kept the scullery clean and I would do the kitchen. Doris also lit and cleaned the kitchen range, which I was overjoyed to hear. I must admit that she made a marvellous job of it, the range really looked quite something; such polished black and burnished steel. She took a real pride in the job too, standing back to admire the effect then giving it another little rub. Like all such ranges, it burned coal and Doris was forever filling the scuttles. As I was bigger and stronger than her, I often used to carry the scuttles in from the coalhouse, but Mrs Buller wasn't altogether pleased by this, saying that if we all did each other's work where would we be. With the licence of being only a temporary, I answered that I wouldn't dream of offering to help Mr Hall. Later on, young Fred, the under-gardener, would often carry them in for me if he saw me struggling, which I suppose bore out the cook's theory that you should stick strictly to your own sphere of work.

My first evening there wasn't too arduous, physically or mentally, as there were only just the five of them upstairs for dinner – though they still got through six courses. The main course was fillets of beef, and Mrs Buller, with an air of faint hopefulness, said to me:

'Well, Margaret, I don't suppose you know how to make a Béarnaise sauce to go with the fillets? It is a tricky sauce to make.'

Though I would have preferred not to have to demonstrate my knowledge on that first evening, I did know how to make the sauce and I could see that my value had already risen in the cook's estimation. For the sweet course she'd made a baked lemon soufflé, and she certainly was a dab hand at making them for this one rose above the dish like a balloon. They dined at eight o'clock so by the time that we sat down to our supper – a lovely steak and kidney pie – it was getting late. As usual, we ate in the servants' hall; Doris and I laid the table and brought in the food. Mrs Buller sat at one end of the table and Mr Hall at the other; I reckon they both thought they were at the head of the table. One sensed a faint antagonism between the cook and the butler, although they were meticulously correct in their dealings with each other – except on one occasion, after I'd been there a few weeks. Mr Hall told me off for something, whereupon Mrs Buller intervened saying:

'I'll thank you, Mr Hall, not to admonish my staff, if you have any complaints, come to me.'

Mary said that because the cook had known the family for years – she had worked for Mr Wardham's mother and, incidentally, seemed to be the only person in the house that Mr Wardham had a pleasant word for – the butler felt that she had an advantage over him, as he had only been there for five years.

Up in our bedroom we four younger servants settled down for a good gossip about the family. Mary remarked that Gerald, the son, although he'd been home only a few weeks, had taken quite a shine to Rose, his eyes were always following her around the dining-room. Rose, though blushing a deep red, denied that he took any more interest in her than he did in any of the staff, for how could one of the gentry be interested in the likes of her. Her mum would be horrified at the very idea, because her mum had been in one place only in service all her life until she married, and she still started her letters to this lady with 'Dear Madam', never Mrs Paine. Like Kipling's 'East is East', I said, but the allusion was lost on Rose.

'What does one do on one's free afternoon and evening in this benighted place? I can't see any kind of social life around here and I'm not addicted to country walks. I have always had this feeling that farm animals take an instinctive dislike to me; and they know that I have no rapport with the country.'

'Cor, Margaret, can't you use long words, you are clever,' and Doris gazed at me admiringly.

'She always could,' said Mary; then she added, slightly maliciously, 'trouble is, Margaret can't pronounce them like they do upstairs.'

I pretended to be indignant, but of course Mary was right. An extensive vocabulary was in no way comparable with the right accent.

'Anyway,' Mary went on, 'you have Wednesday off, same as me. We could go to the village hop, it's only three miles away and the buses run every thirty minutes. The dance finishes at ten o'clock so it's not as though we'd have to leave while it's in full swing. Course, it's not like a proper dance hall; rough floor and just a piano and drums, but at least there's nearly as many males as females so you don't have to lay on the flattery knee deep to get a partner.'

'Don't expect any high-toned conversation,' interrupted Rose. 'The last time I was there, my partner talked all the time about muck-raking, horses and all the gory things that went on when cows calved.'

She was right too, as I found on my first evening there. Most of the young men worked on farms and were wearing great clod-hopping boots. They reeked to high heaven of brilliantine which didn't mix well with the farm odours. My perspiring partner – I made allowances for the perspiration as I was a bit hefty to propel around the floor – kept pigs. Although I like pigs in the abstract, an evening devoted to the idiosyncrasies of these animals was not my idea of conversation. When I, never loth to show off, murmured, '. . . and why the sea is boiling hot and whether pigs have wings', he looked blank. I added, impatiently, 'You know, "through the looking-glass".' But if it were possible, he looked even more vacant. Once we were outside the hall, I was somewhat surprised when I found that his porcine preoccupation was the prelude to being held in a rock-hard embrace, with slobbery kisses and grunts that would have done credit to his charges. I hasten to add that not all the village swains were like him.

Doris had to be up by six o'clock, and Mary, Rose and I at six-thirty. At first I wished Doris had slept in our room so that I could actually witness, from the warmth of my bed, somebody having to start work before me, who up to now had always been the first to rise. I'd never have wanted to be a between-maid; it's a hard job having to help the cook in the early mornings and then, after breakfast, having to help the housemaid. My mother had three months at that job and she told me that forever the cook would be blowing the whistle for her to come down, and the housemaid blowing down for her to come up. Doris didn't seem to mind, and neither Mrs Buller nor Annie were tyrants. Nevertheless, it meant she had two bosses.

By the time I came down there was already a roaring fire in the kitchen-range so the bathwater was getting hot. I put a kettle on the gas stove and made tea for us under servants, then a fresh pot at seven o'clock for those august personages, the upper servants. I took a cup upstairs for the cook; Mary took one to Agnes, and Rose left one outside the butler's bedroom. He'd have liked her to bring it in to his room, but Rose had told him her mother would never let her stay in a place where she had to enter a male servant's bedroom. Presumably, as those above stairs were almost sacrosanct, it would have been all right to take a cup into the son's room. At seven-thirty Annie took tea upstairs for Mr and Mrs Wardham, Miss Helen, the daughter, and Miss Sarah, the niece. The valet, Mr Burrows, did the same for the son.

By seven-thirty I'd laid up the cook's table with all the things she needed for cooking breakfast for us and upstairs, and Doris had laid the table in the servants' hall. We had a good breakfast of porridge, which had been cooked overnight and left to keep warm on the stove, and bacon and eggs. Doris and I had to dish everything out on to the plates, so there wasn't the same formality as there was for midday lunch, when the butler solemnly carved the joint and the vegetables were passed up and down the table in strict pecking order. Our official breakfast time was from eight o'clock until eight forty-five. Upstairs, it was at nine-fifteen. I was pleased to discover that the servants didn't have to assemble upstairs for prayers. And later on, when I caught sight of Mr Wardham's sour-looking face and heard his harsh and overbearing voice, I could tell that it would have been incongruous for him to orate about how we were loved by the One above when it was obvious that the one above, who paid us our wages, didn't even like us.

It rather grieved Mrs Buller that no prayers were said in that house. She considered that to have fifteen minutes of spiritual communion was to start the day well; though as Doris and I said – only to each other of course – as we'd already been up for a couple of hours of hard work without spiritual communion, we could continue to manage without it. But Mrs Buller appeared to be on almost familiar terms with God. Casting her eyes upward, she always spoke of Him as the 'Master'. I got extremely confused about this owing to the fact that when she was working for Mr Wardham's mother, Mr Wardham was always known to her as Master Edward. Now that she worked for him, she referred to him as the Master. Once, when Mrs Buller admonished Doris to hurry with stoking up the range for dinner, the Master didn't like to be kept waiting, I whispered to her that he'd been waiting for hundreds of years so a bit longer wouldn't matter. And besides, I thought, one stoked up for 'him below'. Doris giggled so much that Mrs Buller enquired sarcastically whether we thought we were in training to be cooks or a couple of comics on the stage; and Mr Hall, a balding man of fifty who occasionally tried to be avuncular with the young servants, said, 'Ah, Mrs Buller, when they get to our age they'll realise that "life is real, life is earnest", which drew no response from Cook, who disliked any mention of age. I thought that Mr Hall was being very tactful for Cook must have been ten years older than he was. The only person allowed to be jokey with Mrs Buller was young Fred, the under gardener.

4

On my first morning at Redlands – the name of the house – I
realised that Mary had spoken the truth about Madam. Mrs
Wardham was a rather sad-looking lady, but so very pleasant. She
actually called me Margaret and thanked me for helping them out
at such short notice. Mrs Buller sniffed audibly on hearing this but
I didn't let that detract from my pleasure. I really felt for a few mo-
ments that I was just as important in the scheme of things as the
upper servants. Subsequent remarks from Cook and the butler soon
dispelled such ideas. Not that Mrs Buller was ever really unkind. For
one thing, an experienced kitchenmaid such as I was could lighten
a cook's load of work considerably. After reading the menu, I knew
just what utensils she would require on the kitchen table. And I
knew just what was within my capacity to cook. As Mr Wardham
was only in to lunch at weekends, the meal for them upstairs, unless
there were guests was a simple affair of two courses and cheese. But
a lot of food had to be cooked for our dinner, which was our main
meal at two o'clock, for as well as the nine servants in the house,
both gardeners and the chauffeur sat down with us. Proper ritual
it was too. The cook and butler were ensconced at each end of the
table, Agnes and Violetta each side of Cook, Mr Burrows, the valet,
and Jack, the chauffeur, each side of the butler, and the rest of us in

between. It was my job to lay the table with a huge white cloth, and we all had serviettes rolled up in different coloured rings. It was difficult at first remembering the right places at table to put them – not that it mattered with Fred, the gardener or the chauffeur, as they never bothered to use theirs. Doris and I had to bring in the hot plates, vegetables, gravy and sauce. By the time we all sat down it was quite an impressive sight. Once, young Fred whispered to me, 'You'd think we were in training for the State Banquet,' which caused me to giggle and Mr Hall to frown. If I forgot some item for the table, such as the salt, or enough tablespoons, Mr Hall, as was the way with most butlers, would not address me directly but, looking very grave, and as though he'd just been given private information on some impending catastrophe, would say to the cook:

'Mrs Buller, I'm afraid that Margaret has forgotten something.'

Very occasionally Mr Hall would be in a jocular mood, and Mary and I reckoned this was when departing guests had given him a substantial tip. Then he'd try to be witty, as on the day I gave him the wrong coloured serviette ring.

'Ah, Mrs Buller, what a pity that Margaret is colour-blind.'

Mrs Buller was very nice in that she'd never tell me off in front of the servants, but would have a word with me in private to try not to give Mr Hall any chance to complain.

The under-gardener, a good-looking twenty-year-old, was known as 'young Fred', to distinguish him from his uncle Fred, the head gardener. According to Mary, rumour had it in the village that young Fred was a by-blow of Mr Wardham's. The head gardener's sister had worked as a housemaid for Mr Wardham's mother and had married rather hurriedly the village postman. Young Fred bore no facial resemblance to Mr Wardham and probably the rumours originated in the fact that he had paid for young Fred to have two years' training in horticulture – much to the disgust of Fred, who had natural green fingers and didn't believe in new-fangled methods of gardening. Fred, like a lot of old gardeners who had tended the same garden for years, was extremely possessive about his products. He didn't mind young Fred cutting and uprooting the vegetables for the kitchen, but when it was a question of flowers for upstairs, only he should cut them; and even then, unless Mrs Wardham asked him personally, he was very grudging in the amount he cut. Years of stooping had made his back permanently bowed, and to see him trudging along the road to his home in the village always reminded me of 'the ploughman homeward plods his weary way'.

Young Fred, perhaps owing to his horticultural training, spoke in a far more refined voice than did the village lads. It says much for his likeable personality that his mates never resented what they termed his 'la-di-da voice'. I liked him very much, but although he often kissed me – in the coal-shed of all romantic places – I was sensible enough to know that he meant nothing serious; half the village girls were in love with him. Besides, he also kissed Doris in the coal-shed so I knew he would never be *my* young man.

Young Fred was a great favourite of Mrs Buller's. None of the other men would have dared to make the frivolous remarks to her that he got away with. But then he was a charmer, and that word could never be applied to the butler or the valet, or even to Jack the chauffeur – not unless one was a female on the last gasp for any kind of man. I think the valet was the only person who didn't like young Fred; the reason being that occasionally Fred got articles of clothing from Mr Wardham. Mr Burrows considered that his job as a valet entitled him to any cast-offs. I still remember the day when young Fred was given a pair of almost new brown boots, because they squeaked. He came into the servants' hall just before our dinner time, when all the servants were assembled, and squeak, squeak, squeak went those boots as young Fred walked, quite unnecessarily, round and round the room. Poor Mr Burrows' face got redder and redder and his food nearly choked him. Afterwards, Cook remonstrated with young Fred, saying he'd been unkind and embarrassing to the valet; but that irrepressible young man was in no way abashed.

'I'll tell you what, dear Madam Beeton,' and he grinned merrily, 'tomorrow I'll come in carrying the boots under my arm.'

And did she frown? She did not, but set to and made him his favourite 'seedy' cake for tea.

Our five o'clock tea was the most relaxed time of the day, for unless there had been a special lunch upstairs, most of us had been able to have an hour or two's rest in our rooms. Furthermore, we never ate in formal style around the table but just sat around haphazardly – well, perhaps not quite like that, as certain chairs were sacrosanct to Cook and the butler. It was always the under housemaid's task to get tea for the servants, so I could sit down and watch Mary rushing around from kitchen to servants' hall – quite a long walk, incidentally, along stone-flagged corridors. We nearly always had fruit cake, and even now I still remember how rich and moist it was. Mrs Buller was a dab-hand at making cakes, bread too, everything was home-made. The tea was strong and black because Mr Hall liked it that way. Just like the way Mother made it for my father if he was in work, and if she had the money. When it was weak tea, my father would say, 'What's this then? Water bewitched and tea begrudged.'

At tea-time, Mr Hall and Mr Burrows would discuss our employer; what a foul disposition he had, bullying his wife and daughter and being barely polite to his son. Mrs Buller, out of a kind of loyalty to Mr Wardham's parents – who'd been very good to her – seldom joined in their conversation; but even she had to admit that the master had changed considerably from the boy she had known as Master Edward. Mr Wardham was particularly disagreeable to Miss Helen, his daughter, telling her for God's sake to put a smile on her face and stop mooning around like a love-sick cow. Poor Miss Helen's fiancé had been killed in the last month of the First World War. They were to have been married on his next leave. She'd never recovered from the shock of losing the man she'd loved and been engaged to for three years. Nowadays, no woman of her age would stay at home to be bullied by her father; but it wasn't easy then for an unmarried daughter to be independent. Miss Helen had no income of her own, hadn't been brought up to work and, further-more, was rather plain.

For three years she had been writing a book about war heroes but unfortunately, now it was finished, no publisher would accept it. I thought it very sad that all her work should be unappreciated. At that time I was unaware that the world was full of authors who all considered they had written masterpieces.

After the butler and valet had finished discussing Mr Wardham, they'd talk about previous employers, The valet – as I noticed with most personal servants – invariably related how illustrious were the people he'd worked for and how much they'd thought of him. One couldn't help wondering why he'd ever left such a servant's para-dise. The usual excuse was that the marvellous employers were go-ing abroad. Mrs Buller was fond of talking about death, especially her late husband's – though he hadn't died, merely 'passed over'. The way she described the manner of his dying, well, the 'death of Nelson' was as nothing to the passing away of Mr Buller.

They'd been butler and cook together in a place where the Mas-ter and Madam had thought the world of them. So much so that when the Master was dying, he'd insisted on having Mr Buller round his death-bed with his other friends. Madam died soon after of a broken heart. I noticed that no such fate had overtaken cook after Mr Buller's death. She always referred to him as 'one of nature's gentlmen', and when he 'passed away', he undoubtedly went straight to heaven – where, Mary whispered irreverently, he was probably flying around waiting on the archangels, having worked only for the best people down below.

I'd been at Redlands a week when they had the first dinner party; This also was the very first occasion of the son, Gerald, coming into our domain when there was a no necessity for him to do so. The dinner was given for Miss Sarah, the niece; and eleven people had been invited, making sixteen in all. Doris and I had no time to gos-sip on that day, especially as Mrs Buller was slightly irritable with all the preparation of the food. Though she wasn't so rancorous as old Fred when he saw his flower-beds denuded for the vases.

There were caviar canapés, followed by chestnut soup. This involved rubbing pounds of cooked chestnuts through a fine sieve – not a job I would recommend if one is in a hurry. The third course was salmon maître d'hotel, then the entrée, sweetbreads en caisse – and I made that dish. The main course was sirloin of beef and, thank heavens, Doris had to grate the stick of horseradish – it's worse than onions for making one's eyes stream with water. There was a cold sweet, a charlotte russe; and the last course, the savoury, was cheese aigrettes. That finished our work; the butler had to look after the Stilton cheese and the dessert. Doris and I were faced with mounds of washing-up and by the time we'd finished, and Mr Hall and Rose had cleared the dining-room, it was eleven o'clock when we sat down to our supper of cold ham, jacket potatoes and salad. We were just having a cup of tea before finishing the tidy-up when, to our astonishment – and the displeasure of the upper servants – the son came into our servants' hall. Such an event was unheard of. Occasionally those above stairs would come into the kitchen on some pretext, but never into the servants' hall; that was our private domain.

Master Gerald knocked on the door, came right in and said, 'The dinner was splendid. You all worked so hard and I'm sure must be very tired.' Then, turning to the valet, he added, 'Burrows, you needn't do anything for me tomorrow morning, I'll look after myself. Goodnight to you all.'

Far from being gratified at hearing this praise, there was an uneasy silence after the son had gone. Then Mr Hall spoke, to nods of agreement from Cook, Agnes and Mr Burrows.

'Why should he come into our place without so much as a 'by your leave'. If anyone is going to say thank you, it should be Master or Madam, not that Gerald. And I don't know if you noticed it Mrs Buller, but I didn't like the way that he looked at Rose. It's not the way a gentleman should look at a young servant girl.'

Rose blushed a vivid red and kept silent. Mr Burrows, who should have been pleased that he'd only Mr Wardham to valet, said, in an aggrieved voice, 'Mr Hall, did you ever hear the like? Look after himself indeed. To say that to me, who's valeted the best in the land.'

When we were in our bedroom Mary and I agreed that Mr Hall was really annoyed because Gerald – we dropped the 'master' when nobody was around – had looked at Rose instead of at him. Though, come to that, we were secretly a bit chagrined that he'd ignored us and we lost no time in telling Rose that Gerald would have forgotten about her in the morning.

I think everybody must have liked Mrs Wardham as she was really kind and thoughtful. Talking to Cook the following morning, she said that they would all be out to dinner so perhaps the young girls, that was Mary, Rose, Doris and I, would like to go to the village dance. Although it was Madam who'd suggested it, we all had to be suitably grateful to the upper servants for their graciousness in letting us have an extra evening off. Agnes, a spinster of about forty-five, told Mary that no such treats had ever come her way when she was an under-housemaid; and Mr Hall told Rose that he'd planned to check the silver room and clean any tarnished pieces but, and he patted her on the shoulder with his white lardy hands, he'd do the work on his own.

The dance started at seven o'clock and we began to get ready about two hours before that. For, unlike town dances, at the village hops everybody arrived almost as soon as the musicians; they made sure of getting their money's worth. With Rose's natural advantages, it didn't take her long to get ready. Her lovely glossy golden hair never needed curling, whereas we tortured ours with 'dinky' curlers and then proceeded to comb it into a mass of frizz. Make-up consisted of a liberal layer of pink powder. We never dared to use coloured lipstick, only 'that sort of a woman' would use it, so we rubbed our lips with a lip salve to make them shiny. Several dabs of 4711 eau de Cologne completed our toilet. Although Rose made us look plainer by comparison, having her with us did ensure that we got some partners. While the village youths were waiting their turn to be her partner, they'd take us round the floor just so they could be attached to our party. We weren't quite accepted by the older generation because none of us were locals. I suppose for some twenty-five miles around, the large houses were mostly staffed by village girls whose mothers and grandmothers had also been in service there. But, according to Cook, Mr Wardham refused to employ any local girls who'd go home and gossip about his household all over the village. So, as he wasn't popular, we too were regarded as outsiders.

Young Fred was at the dance, Jack, the chauffeur, and his wife, and Jack's father who, when he'd had a few beers – which happened frequently – would bitterly inveigh against 'this new-fangled transport', the motor car. He was an 'orses man and his father had been an 'orses man. There wasn't nothing to beat an 'orse. It didn't make 'orrible noises and stink up the roads with smoke so that decent country folk got poisoned with the fumes, God's clean air had gone and all the flowers had died. Give 'im an 'orse any time. One could easily tell that Jack's father had been an 'orse man. His legs were so bowed one could have driven a pig to market through them.

Young Fred seldom danced with Rose; he said that she 'hadn't got what it takes upstairs'. That didn't mean, as it would nowadays, that she wasn't any good in bed, but that she wasn't very intelligent. I protested that Rose was merely quiet. As an only child, she'd been very suppressed by her parents, allowed to be seen but not heard, and she was naturally shy. I wondered if young Fred was jealous of Rose, when he laughed and said rather cynically:

'Shy! She's not exactly blushing unseen and wasting her sweetness on the desert air.'

'Why should she? And you're no village Hampden, defying some little tyrant either.'

'*Elegy in a Country Churchyard*' we said simultaneously, and spent some time quoting extracts; much to the annoyance of the village girls who wanted to dance with him. Young Fred and two other swains escorted us back; poor Doris was the odd one out but she didn't seem to mind in the least. At the beginning of the drive we all said goodbye to our young men and I could hear giggling and 'don't you dare' from Mary and Rose. Young Fred said he had liked talking to me, but personally I'd have derived far more pleasure and satisfaction if he had seized me in a violent embrace and kissed me passionately. A good brain was something but a lovely face would have earned more in dividends. We'd nearly reached the path leading to the servants' entrance when, all of a sudden, we saw Gerald coming down the drive towards us. We stopped, surprised and embarrassed. He asked if we'd enjoyed the evening and then, looking at Rose, said, 'I'm sure that you were the belle of the ball'. None of us spoke, we were too dumbfounded, and he walked on towards the end of the drive. We waited for a few minutes, then whispered to each other that we'd not mention the episode to the upper servants, they'd be sure to blame us.

We still looked flustered when we went into our servants' hall, but I suppose Cook and the butler put it down to the heat of the dance. We had to listen to Cook telling us that she was twenty-five before she went to a dance. Dear Mr Buller – one of nature's gentlemen – had taken her; and when he'd brought her home he'd stood on her mother's doorstep, bowed, and kissed her hand 'just as though I was a real lady'. In fact, they'd been courting for three months before he asked permission to kiss her. We endeavoured to suppress our smiles, but in our bedroom we agreed that the late Mr Buller must have been a pretty poor specimen of a male. Then, thinking that Mrs Buller's moustache might even then have been incipient, we invented various reasons why dear Mr Buller wouldn't have been madly inclined to kiss her. Doris made us laugh even more by saying there was a seventeen-year-old girl at the orphanage who hadn't any hair at all; not on her head, under her arms or down below. But it wasn't the poor girl's bald head that the matron cared about, it was the baldness down below; matron said it was indecent. Poor Doris, who'd been sent to the orphanage when she was only four years old, had received very little in the way of love and care as a child. In her last two years at the orphanage she worked long hours in the laundry. She still worked hard but at least she always had enough to eat; and Cook, although sharp-tongued occasionally, was never really unkind.

5

Cook was certainly in a bad mood on the morning following our dance. This was partly caused by the master wanting an early breakfast, eight o'clock instead of nine. Cook disliked having breakfast time altered, she said it threw her out for the rest of the day. Besides, how could she get the servants' breakfast and cook for upstairs at the same time. Breakfast for upstairs was no simple matter of bacon and eggs. As well as the porridge, which had kept warm on the stove overnight, there were sausages, kidneys, bacon, eggs and often kedgeree as well. I used to wonder how it was that our employers never become inordinately fat on such a diet, but they seemed to keep their figures. Mrs Buller was also put out because of the upheaval in the scullery. The old smelly cement sink was being knocked out and a lovely deep, yellow glazed one put in. Needless to say, Doris and I were delighted for it was we who'd had to use the foul-smelling grey sink. Two plumbers from the village came, early in the morning, and promised to get it finished that day. Unfortunately, as the only other sink was in the butler's pantry, we had to use it for all the washing-up. The fuss that Mr Hall made about having his pantry invaded by kitchen servants, you'd have thought we were suffering from some contagious disease. He refused to have Doris in there as well as me so I had to do all the washing-up. What was more, I had to wait to do it until he and Rose had done all the cutlery and glasses. Relations were quite strained between him and Cook, especially after he complained about me 'splashing-up his draining-boards.'

'Mr Hall,' said Cook, ultra politely, 'I'm sure I have no wish to inconvenience you in any way, but do you expect my girls to wash up in buckets of water in the yard? We are all on this earth to help one another, and live by the good Book.'

Mr Hall walked out of the kitchen without saying a word but, if the expression on his face was anything to go by, he certainly wasn't living by the 'good Book.' Actually, the only books he ever read were lurid detective stories. He'd got most of Sax Rohmer's; *Dr Fu Manchu, The Yellow Claw* and others. I suppose those tales of the mysterious orient compensated for his own somewhat dull existence. Apart from the Bible, Cook had only four books which she read over and over again. A book called, *Stepping Stones to Bible History*; then there was *East Lynne, Little Women* and *Little Lord Fauntleroy*. This last one, carefully covered in brown paper, she lent to me, and Rose, and Mary and I giggled at that impossible youth calling his mother 'Dearest'. Rose said she couldn't imagine what her mum would say if Rose called her Dearest. Why, she'd never even heard her father say 'Dear', let alone Dearest.

Cook was very pious but, as Mary and I agreed, for a pious person she seemed to know of a great many girls who were now 'living in sin'. All because they had left their quiet village homes for the lights of London. According to Mrs Buller, there were always harpies waiting at the railway stations ready to lure away innocent girls if they were at all pretty. This fate could never have happened to Cook – come to that, nor to me either. I'd never seen anybody remotely resembling a harpy hanging around Victoria Station. Doris asked what a harpy was, and Mr Hall was just about to give his version of a harpy when, ever eager to show off, I interrupted to say that a harpy was a monster, half bird, half woman. That a kitchen-maid should interrupt the butler was a heinous offence.

Mr Hall gave me a freezing look and, in his 'upstairs' voice, said;

'Perhaps Miss Know-all would care to regale us with some further information about monsters? I'm sure she must have met many in the course of her long life.'

I'd have liked to have retorted, 'Yes, and some of them were butlers too,' but of course I didn't dare.

Fortunately, by the time we sat down to our midday dinner, Cook and the butler were friendly again. Mr Burrows was still displeased about Master Gerald not requiring his services, he felt this as a slight on his profession.

'Man and boy, I've been in service and valeted some of the highest aristocracy in the land. Why, in my last place, my gentleman consulted me every morning about what suit and tie he should wear. "Burrows", he'd say, "today I'm lunching with Lord . . .", and when I'd laid out the appropriate clothes, hat, shoes and umbrella, my gentleman said, "Burrows, you are indeed a gentleman's gentleman".'

Young Fred hooted with laughter, and it did sound a highly improbable remark. The butler, not to be outdone in reminiscences of above stairs benevolence related how, in *his* last place, an American guest had been so overcome with admiration at the way Mr Hall carried out his butlering duties, he'd tried to entice him to go back to America with him; and he'd pay twice the money his present gentleman was paying.

'But, needless to say,' Mr Hall went on loftily, 'I just wouldn't serve in an American household. They've no idea of how to behave with servants. You may not belive this, but that American kept on calling me "old chap". I ask you, what kind of a gentleman is that?'

Probably a very nice one, I thought to myself. . . .

6

By the time I'd been at Redlands a month there was still no sign of Mrs Buller's niece taking over as kitchen maid, so I had my day off. It really was a marvellous surprise to find that one got the whole day free, and did not even have to do the breakfast. Doris, who had no relatives and nowhere to go, hadn't taken her day off; and though I'd urged her to stay in her room she preferred to work.

As it was Mary's free day too, we decided to go to London. We had to listen to solemn advice from Cook about not talking to strange men, but I had no men friends so if I didn't talk to strange ones I'd never talk to any. Cook seemed to forget that I'd worked in London, or perhaps she thought a month of rustic life had lulled my sense of the dangers in a city.

We got an early bus into Southampton and found it was full of men on their way to work, so that in itself was an adventure; very seldom had we ever found ourselves in a situation where men outnumbered the females. Mary and I made the most of this rare occurrence; by the time the bus journey ended, we'd promised to meet two of them on our next free evening. We felt quite safe for we knew they'd have forgotten all about us by then – and probably they were already married.

There were only females in the No Smoking compartments so we gave them a miss. As Mary said, better to be smoke-dried with the men than bored to death with the Aunt Agatha's. In 1925 very few women smoked, and almost none at all in public. It was a well-known fact that if a woman did such a thing, decent men avoided her like the plague – though considering the scarcity of men who showed any desire for us, we might as well have smoked ourselves to death.

We looked around for harpies at Waterloo station but nobody approached us, even though we were dressed in our best clothes. We decided it was too early in the day; harpies were probably sleeping off the previous evening's orgy.

We went into a Lyons teashop and had bacon and sausages; what a treat to be waited on by a smart and pleasant nippy instead of us having to do the waiting. We left her twopence for a tip and thought we were really big spenders. Selfridge's was the next treat, and we wandered around working out just what we'd buy if we had £50 to spend. As Mary had only £5, and I even less, such flights of fancy got us nowhere. We bought Doris a necklace of gaudy glass beads, and Agnes a small remnant of material so that she could continue to make useless knick-knacks, such as 'hair tidies' and pin-cushions. For Rose we bought a hair-slide, and for cook a religious book-marker with the proverb, 'A soft answer turneth away wrath, but a grievous word stirreth up anger'. Hopefully, whenever Doris and I made a mistake, she'd remember those words and take a deep breath instead of getting irate. In the chemist's we bought some Phul-Nana violet cachous so that we could breathe romantically over any young man, should an opportunity to do so arise. And on the chemist's counter we saw bottles of tablets labelled REVITALISERS. I'd have liked to have bought a bottle for the butler but knew he'd be highly affronted. Besides, as Mary pointed out, the result of any revitalising wouldn't reveal itself in our direction, even if we could overlook the corporation and bald head. Mr Hall seemed to be totally indifferent to females, even to Rose. His free evenings were generally spent in the saloon bar of the local with two or three other butlers from the manor houses in other villages. There, according to young Fred from his vantage point in the public bar, they'd talk gravely about the fads and foibles of their employers, how the running of the house would be a shambles if it wasn't for their butlering, what high class guests they'd served at dinner – and what tips they'd been handed out. Quite a few of the guests, though high in blue blood, were low in money; and as they did the rounds of being guests at country houses, their style of tipping was known in advance to the butlers and valets. As none of these tips, whether high or low, were ever distributed to the kitchen staff, we had no interest in the matter.

I managed to get Mary into the British Museum – one of my favourite haunts when in London – but she quickly got bored with the place. I just couldn't see how anybody could be bored with the variety of wonderful and beautiful objects to see there.

'It's all free,' I told Mary, 'We could spend hours in here and it wouldn't cost us a penny. Where else could you do that, I'd like to know?'

'Free, Margaret! Sure, it's free on your pocket but that's about the lot. Half an hour wandering about and my feet are killing me; if you raise your voice or laugh people look at you as though you've crawled out from under a stone; and the attendants watch you as though you and the treasures will disappear together. Free! I wouldn't cross the road and pay twopence to see the place.'

So that finished the British Museum for us. And it was a good job we didn't have to pay for with Mary I'd never have got my money's worth. Portobello Road was more to Mary's taste. In those days the stalls were full of tattered and torn books with obscure titles that I'd never heard of – any pictures in them had long since been torn out. There were old clothes that looked as though they'd been shot at, and stalls filled with junk such as chipped and cracked china, rusty fire-irons and old door-handles. There was not the same craze for antiques then as there is now; one which has crowded the markets, sent prices soaring and brought a bonanza to stall holders. I bought for threepence a large chipped mug painted with a scene of

Margate Pier and the words A PRESENT FROM MARGATE. It could be a shaving mug for my father, though Mary said what on earth would he want with a present from Margate when he lived in Hove. Not that Dad ever did get it as I broke it before I went home. Mary bought a small coloured picture of a gold-braided bearded naval officer; she said it reminded her of her absent Tom. Thought as her young man was only an AB, and clean-shaven, I'd have thought the likeness purely imaginary. Still, anything that reminded her she had an 'understanding' could only be a good thing. For ninepence in the cinema, ordinary dull life vanished while we watched handsome and dashing Douglas Fairbanks in *The Three Musketeers* – I think he was D'Artagnan. When we came out, Mary sighed and said wouldn't it be wonderful if there were men like that now, and in England. She sighed even more when I said that even if there were, we certainly wouldn't find them in domestic service; even the wildest flights of fancy could never see the butler and valet as dashing swordsmen. The only implement that Mr Hall flashed around was a silver salver, and Mr Burrows the clothes-brush.

'We should have gone to the pictures later in the day,' Mary complained, 'We might have been lucky enough to sit next to a couple of young men instead of those elderly females.'

'What good would that have done us, Mary? Even though Jack's meeting us at Southampton, we've still got to leave before nine o'clock. We'd hardly have time to enamour them with our charms so that they'd come all the way to Southampton to see us on our free evening.'

'You're right as usual, Margaret. Let's go to Paddington and see if my aunt's indoors. She's a waitress at Lyons Corner House and does shift work.'

Mary's aunt lived in a street near the Grand Union Canal. She was the youngest of a family of ten children and, so Mary had heard from her mother, the only one that had ever brought disgrace on the family. For generations, the Howards in their Norfolk village, had been respectable farmers, never a breath of scandal had blown over them. Now their Elly, the youngest, had disgraced them by becoming pregnant. And with a travelling tinker too, who had left the village never to be heard of again. If it had been some local boy he could have been made to marry their Elly. So she was turned out of her home by an irate and outraged father, and with £50 surreptitiously given by her mother Elly went to London and had the baby, which lived only a few hours.

We found Mary's Aunt Elly in the middle of packing. Her appearance certainly was a surprise to me. We were wearing dresses that came just below our knees but Aunt Elly's dress was not only form-fitting, but ended just *above* the knees. Her hair wasn't merely bobbed, it was cut in a very short style that was to become fashionable about two years later – known as the Eton Crop.

She welcomed us into her large bedsitter and offered us tea or sherry. We chose the latter. We could drink tea anytime but sherry was really something.

'You moving, Aunt Elly?' asked Mary.

'Yes, ducky. I'm getting married.'

'Getting married?' We both uttered this in startled voices as though it was an unheard of event. I suppose Aunt Elly was only about thirty-five, but to us that seemed far too old for anybody to want to marry her.

She laughed at our astonishment, saying, 'And why shouldn't I? I'm pretty easy on the eye' And that was true, she was very attractive.

'I'm marrying one of the regular customers at my tables. He's a widower of sixty, retired and no children, fortunately. He's lonely and I'm fed up working for miserable wages and always expected to be nice and smiling to the customers. Eric's nothing to look at, and his idea of witty conversation is seaside postcard jokes, but he's got money and is kind and generous. We're going to travel abroad for a year and then settle down in his house in Bournemouth, where he says his wife made love on a strictly descending scale. When first they were married it was a weekly occasion, then a monthly one; and during their last few years together they made love only once a year – and if she could have made it every leap year that would have

31

suited her fine.' Here, Aunt Elly looked really wicked as she added, 'He's got a few surprises in store when he gets into bed with me. I'll soon have him in good condition.'

Mary and I thought her aunt was really quite somebody and wished that we too could be so lucky. Though, as Mary remarked on the way back, one would need to drink a lot of sherry to feel like getting into bed with an old man of sixty. Still, at that, he might have in quality what he lacked in quantity, and in any case a lot of money does enable one to suffer in comfort.

Jack, the chauffeur, had asked Madam if he could use the car to pick us up at the station. He knew it was no use asking Mr Wardham, who disliked his own family and certainly wouldn't have done a kindness to the servants. So we drove back to Redlands in great style, sucking our cachous in case our breath smelt of the sherry. But we found the upper servants too preoccupied and uneasy to worry about us, and Rose and Doris had gone to bed. Cook gave us our supper and hurried us upstairs. She was the only one to ask us if we'd enjoyed our day.

Cook was sensible enough to refrain from saying we were not to gossip in our bedroom, though we generally spoke very quietly as she slept on the same floor. The butler and valet had their bedrooms in the basement. Sensing that some untoward event had happened in our absence, Mary and I were all agog to hear the news. We found Doris sitting on Rose's bed and both waiting for us.

'Oh, Margaret!' burst out Doris, 'you should have been here today, you'd have loved it. If you'd seen Mr Hall's and Mr Burrows' faces, cor it was a real treat, better than the pictures.'

'Don't sit there babbling, tell us what happened. You tell us, Rose,' said Mary impatiently.

So Rose told us that the first event had taken place while they were having their tea. Miss Helen, as nice and kind a person as her mother, had knocked on the door of the servants' hall and asked if she might come in. She was collecting information on old country houses and wanted to know if any of them had worked in notable places and had any stories or incidents to relate. Agnes said that her mother had been a housemaid in a place called Marston Manor, and that it was supposed to be haunted by the ghost of a lady who'd been murdered by her husband. And Cook said that she didn't think any of the houses where she'd been in service were notable, but that when she started as scullery maid around 1885 in Kensington, she always got the shivers when she went into the coal-cellar – as though a cold wind was blowing on her.

'Probably the draught coming through the coal-hole cover in the pavement,' I interrupted, but then Doris hastened to continue.

'Oh, Margaret, if you'd been there. You know how Mr Hall and Mr Burrows are always on about the posh houses they've worked in, "highest in the land", Mr Hall is always telling us. Well, when Miss Helen asked them, they went red in the face and Mr Hall said he'd worked for Sir William Price, who was now living in America – and I've never heard of him, have you? – and the house was called Longton Hall and had a tower built on the end and, would you believe it, Margaret, that was the only place he could think of.'

'As for Mr Burrows,' Rose added, 'he couldn't think of any notable place at all except some old Colonel's who was now in India, and he thought the country mansion had been destroyed by fire.'

'Serve them right,' laughed Mary. 'Perhaps we won't have to listen again to all their boring tales of past situations. But what else happened?'

Rose blushed and looked embarrassed, but also as though she was secretly pleased. And we heard that Mr Gerald had come down into the basement around nine o'clock, just as dinner was over. He was wearing a dinner-jacket, and had a button in his hand which he said had just come of the jacket – Mr Hall reckoned he'd pulled it off. He'd wanted Rose to sew it on, but Mr Hall had intervened saying it was Burrows' job to take care of Mr Gerald's clothes; Rose was a parlour maid. Mr Gerald had insisted that he wanted Rose to do it and had told Mr Hall that rigid spheres of work were outdated, and in Rhodesia all the whites were equal and there was none of this Sir and Madam. White people weren't servants, he'd said, they had the blacks for that. Despite Mr Hall's disapproval, Rose had sewn the button on; and Mr Gerald said what nice slender fingers she had, and where did she live and was she engaged. All of this enraged Mr Hall exceedingly, and when they were having supper he actually swore – and he'd never done that before in front of the female servants.

'Who's he?' Mr Hall had said, red with anger, 'to come down into our place talking about what he did in Rhodesia. Course they don't have white servants when they've got all those bloody blacks who work for next to nothing. Who does he think he is coming down here and expecting my Rose' – as though Rose was Mr Hall's property – 'to do a job that it's not her place to do? I've never seen the like. I reckon being out there three years he's forgotten what an English gentleman's like. They've got their place upstairs and we've got ours down here, and that's how it should be.'

'Lord help us,' said Cook, 'If it happens again, my advice to you, Mr Hall, is to mention the matter to the Master.'

She meant Mr Wardham, not the Master up in heaven. I don't think the butler did much communing with the One above.

'Did anybody say anything to you Rose?' asked Mary.

'Only Violette, and you know how she talks in her own language when she's excited. She gabbled on and all we understood was the bit at the end, *Rose est une belle jeune fille*. And that didn't please our Mr Hall. Pompously he quoted, "Handsome is as handsome does," and Rose had no call to go against me. I really felt awful when he said that.'

I was just about to say that I reckoned Mr Hall was jealous that an under servant should be personally noticed by one of them above stairs, when Mrs Buller knocked on our door and told us to get off to sleep.

The subject wasn't mentioned at our breakfast the next morning; but that meal was seldom enlivened by conversation, the butler and cook being particularly sharp-tongued early in the day. I generally woke in a cheerful mood and, knowing Mrs Buller's religious tendencies, I used to sing hymns. One morning I was singing 'Awake my soul and with the sun thy daily stage of duty run', when Cook interrupted me saying there was a time and place for everything and personally she preferred to listen to hymns in the proper surroundings. I'd have liked to answer that I thought hymns could be sung anywhere, but after one look at Cook's face I knew it wouldn't be politic.

In any case, Cook hurried with the breakfast as there was to be a lunch party upstairs for ten people. I remember seeing Mrs Wardham coming into the kitchen to give the orders for the day; she looked so tired and sad and yet she managed a smile and a kind word for Doris and me. Mrs Buller cooked a braised saddle of veal and delicious it was too served with a rich gravy flavoured with claret. Naturally the redcurrant jelly was home-made. It was my job to cook the vegetables, one of which was creamed spinach. This involved cooking about four pounds of the stuff, rubbing it through a wire sieve – a very tedious task – and then reheating the spinach with butter and cream; I must say it did taste good. For the sweet, cook had made a gateau St Honoré. Awful lot of work to make and decorate, but she said that the finished result was worth the trouble. I suppose it was, but I thought of all that time and trouble being consumed in a matter of minutes.

Having a luncheon party upstairs meant that our dinner was late; much to the annoyance of Fred who's only interest in life seemed to be his gardening and his food. Young Fred told us that his uncle, as a young man, had been a great one for the girls, a proper village Lothario. One needed a very vivid imagination to picture toothless old Fred in that role, and certainly I reckoned he was long past it now – his bent back alone presenting certain difficulties in bed. Mrs Buller had warned Doris and me not to mention the subject of Rose and Mr Gerald; but it was just an ordinary remark by me that sparked off dissension at the dinnertable. Mrs Buller had roasted a leg of mutton for us with all the trimmings, roast potatoes, peas, onion sauce and mint sauce. I whispered to Mary how nice it was to have as good food as they had upstairs, so different from my last place where conditions had been so bad it was enough to turn all the servants socialist. Mr Hall, and one had only to look at his face to see that yesterday's event was still rankling, overheard me and said to Cook, in a very sour voice.

'Did you hear that, Mrs Buller? Margaret likes the Socialists. No doubt she sees herself as another Margaret Bondfield in a Labour Government – and they didn't last long, did they? Maybe Margaret would like to fraternise with Mr Gerald who seems to have the same ideas. Perhaps she could do his washing.'

'What's all that about?' asked young Fred.

So then it all came out about Mr Gerald and Rose. Young Fred said why shouldn't Mr. Gerald talk to Rose if he wanted to. People like him had fallen for working-class girls before now. And then young Fred turned to Cook and said what about King Cophetua and the beggarmaid and Cook replied that that had happened in biblical times when people lived the simple life. All right, then, went on Fred, what about King Charles and Nell Gwyn, didn't the king say on his death-bed, 'Don't let poor Nelly starve?' The valet answered, with what I considered irrefutable logic, that he couldn't see the connection, nobody here was contemplating the starving of Rose. Young Fred got really irritated then and pointed out all the actresses that had actually married into the nobility.

Although I didn't much care for the butler, I inwardly agreed with him when he said that was different affair entirely. Actresses were a race apart, extremely glamorous and always in the public eye. Lords and Dukes liked to be seen in their company. But the Wardhams were of very old and aristocratic lineage who'd always married with equally blue blood. Besides, how on earth could a girl like Rose mix with them above stairs? She wasn't well-educated, couldn't tell the difference between a Rembrandt and the picture on a calendar, couldn't speak like them. 'Anyway,' said young Fred, 'Rose is as pretty as any actress.'

All this was going on about Rose just as though she wasn't sitting at the table. But she said never a word one way or the other. I suppose that was the best policy really. It certainly was a policy calculated to annoy Mr Hall who I believe, though not having any amorous inclinations for Rose himself, resented the fact that other men should. Still, as Mary and I agreed later on in our bedroom, we were seeing life in our servants' hall, and learning a bit too.

8

For the next few weeks life was comparatively calm. There was a fair amount of entertaining above stairs and I helped quite a bit in the cooking of sauces and vegetables – the latter always prepared by Doris, fortunately. I actually made a shepherd's pie for our dinner which Mr Hall graciously condescended to tell me direct, was almost as good as Mrs Buller's. I don't think Cook was altogether pleased to hear this, but she did tell me that I was a great help to her – rare praise from any cook.

Mr Gerald came down early one evening – a legitimate reason this time. His father had asked him to go into the wine cellar with Mr Hall to get a bottle of the old port. Even then he lingered in the butler's pantry, though he said nothing directly to Rose. He spoke about the Labour government; that although they'd held office for such a short time, he knew they weren't finished, their time would come again. He was sure that we servants must be proud to know that the son of a Scots farm labourer could rise to be a Prime Minister. It showed that we were all equal – which statement was manifestly untrue; if he'd worked below stairs he'd never have made such an inane remark.

The following day, while we were having dinner, Mr Hall brought up the subject again, saying to Mr Burrows, apropos of the Labour government; 'As for that Ramsay Macdonald, I don't hold with people rising above their station. No good comes of it. It stands to reason he couldn't run the country, he don't know the right kind of people. I've been a Conservative all my life and I'm not putting no working-class man in Westminster to tell me what to do. Besides, from what I've heard the Master say, they've got Communists in their Party and you know what they're like. Look what happened in Russia.'

'What did happen?' asked Doris, but Mr Hall just ignored her.

Young Fred said that at least Ramsay MacDonald had tried to prevent a future war by helping to draft the Geneva Protocol. Mr Hall had never heard of it – and to be honest neither had I. Young Fred and I were discussing the moral principles of war when the valet interrupted our conversation by asking, what could I know about the war, I was only eighteen now. It couldn't have made any difference to me. Only those people who'd actually fought had any idea what war was really like. To which point of view the butler nodded his head and proceeded to tell us a long and boring story about some pal of his who'd got 'trench feet' and never recovered.

Young Fred who, being an outside worker, didn't care two hoots about the butler's opinions, just laughed, saying, 'Well, he wouldn't, would he? He can't get himself another pair of feet. Anyway, Margaret does know about the war. She actually reads books, not lurid Limehouse dramas and the yellow press.'

I rather wished he hadn't said that because I knew it would infuriate Mr Hall and I, unlike young Fred, couldn't get away from him. Anyway, it wasn't true that the First World War meant nothing to me. Although there were few civilian casualties, I remembered it in other ways: such as my father going to France, our greatly increased standard of living when we had three soldiers billeted on us, and the rushing from shop to shop when we heard that they'd found some margarine or fruit.

During last month I had, wonder of wonders, acquired a boyfriend. He was the young man who brought us eggs from a farm.

Lovely eggs they were too, so new-laid they were often still warm. As this young man, Bob by name, came three times a week, he didn't have time to forget me inbetween. As I said to Mary, 'I grow on people.'

'Yes, like a wart,' she replied cynically, but I put that down to pique because she hadn't heard from her sailor boyfriend for some months.

Of course, this Bob's liking for me could have been helped on by the slice of fruit cake I gave him every time he called. Invariably I have found that a man's stomach is of equal importance to him as the affairs of his heart, if not more so. I'm sure if they feel sick for want of food, however lovesick they are, it's the former that takes priority. Cook was now letting me make the cakes for the servants' tea; and as none of them complained they must have been all right.

Gladys, the under-housemaid where I'd been a kitchenmaid in Thurloe Square, used to say to me when we were trying to snaffle two young men, 'All you have to do, Margaret, is find 'em and feed 'em.'

Nowadays there's another four letter word you need to keep them, but it wasn't so then. Oh, a young man would try it on, but when you refused to do anything but kiss him it didn't automatically mean that was the last you'd see of him.

As this Bob wasn't bad-looking, and a good dancer, I promptly gave up going to the village dances; for nothing is more humiliating than being a wallflower, while the boy who has taken you to the dance is gaily cavorting round the floor with some other girl. You go to the dance with your partner, fully determined not to be annoyed or jealous if he dances with somebody else; then, just because you've been lucky enough to actually have a male take you to the affair, you are perhaps besieged by other males, all wanting to dance with you; and they are regardless of the fact that such a longed-for event has never happened to you in your life before. Nor is it ever likely to happen again, considering you're no raving beauty, and when you dance you always seem to have one foot too many. Don't ask me why one has these wild imaginings, one just does; or anyway, I did.

Like the first Sunday afternoon Bob arranged to take me out to tea. Immediately he told me, I had visions of a lovely tea-room with soft lights and sweet music. With my delicate hands – well, perhaps delicate is the wrong word, it's difficult to have 'pale hands I loved beside the Shalimar' when one is a kitchenmaid – I'd pour him dainty cups of tea and we'd have buttered scones and cream cakes, while at the same time I'd intimate that these concoctions, though edible, weren't nearly as good as I could make myself.

But the reality, on a Sunday afternoon in Southampton when all the shops were closed, was a bleak cafe with pink-washed walls, brown linoleum and marble-topped tables, stained with tea and fly-spotted. Alone with me, Bob seemed to have little to say, which perhaps was just as well as I was too distracted by the flying fauna of wasps and flies to pay heed to any conversation. And I thought, as indeed I had often thought, how difficult it is for the poor to be romantic. They have nowhere to go for privacy. If you take a boyfriend home, your family, having only the one sitting-room, are always there. So it's 10p at the pictures, fish and chips in a newspaper, and kissing as far away from a street lamp as possible. It's easy for the rich to have a 'grande passion'; they can dine, drink and dance to induce the mood, and have somewhere to retire for the privacy and pleasure.

About four to five weeks after the sewing-on of a button episode, Rose told Mary and me, in the strictest secrecy, that Mr Gerald wanted to marry her. We immediately felt envious. We knew that she'd been meeting him from time to time; though in fact we'd warned her that he couldn't possibly have honourable intentions. We cited cases, real and imaginary, of girls we'd known in service who'd been seduced by one of the sons or nephews of those upstairs. We painted a harrowing picture of what happened to such girls if they had a baby: they were dismissed instantly without a reference and refused a home by their parents. I even quoted from the *Vicar of Wakefield:*

'When lovely woman stoops to folly
And finds too late that men betray,
What charm can soothe her melancholy,
What art can wash her guilt away?'

But Rose stoutly averred that she would never be seduced; it was marriage or nothing.

'What about that Len your Mum wants you to marry, what's going to happen to him?' asked Mary.

'That's just it, I'm scared to death to tell my ma and pa. Ma's ever so strait-laced and she'd never want one of the gentry for a son-in-law. And as for Pa, he's ever such a Labour man and believes that the workers will never get a living wage until everybody's in a trade union. He says it's people like those we work for that grind the faces of the poor. Can you imagine our dear Madam grinding our faces?'

'Perhaps not, but certainly I can see that old brute her husband doing it,' I said. 'I'm sure he looks upon us as barely literate.'

'Margaret,' broke in Rose, 'it's my day off next week and you haven't had your second day yet. Will you come to my home to back me up when I tell Ma and Pa? I'd be ever so grateful, I really would. I'd let them know that you were coming with me.'

'What! all the way to Manchester? We'd never do it in a day.'

But Rose said that if we started early we'd have a few hours there; long enough to break the news to her parents.

Although Mary and I continued to point out the hazards of life with one above stairs, we were honest enough to admit that had it happened to us we'd have married him like a shot. I don't believe that Rose was really in love, but was dazzled by the prospect of living a life of affluence and becoming one of them above stairs. She couldn't see that she'd never really be one of them; she'd never be able to keep up conversation at a dinner for she never read, not even novels, and knew absolutely nothing about politics or the arts.

9

M y boyfriend, Bob, was annoyed that my day off was going to be spent with Rose. When I told him I was going to Manchester, he was incredulous; you'd have thought Manchester was in the Arctic Circle. But then Bob had never in his life been further than London, and there only on rare occasions. What made it worse was that I couldn't tell him the real reason for going with Rose.

'What d'you want to see her parents for? You don't know them. Besides, I was going to take you to my home, my mum said to bring you in for a bit of supper, she wants to see you.'

Here we go again, I thought. Another mum wanting to give me the once-over. I'd had that before when I knew Percy and met his gorgon of a mother. It needed some female with stronger nerves than mine to wrest that Perce from the loving arms of his mum – in spite of his being thirty years old. Still, perhaps all mothers were the same. I remember my mum, on the rare occasions I brought a boy to Sunday tea, would say the next day, 'Oh yes, Nell. He's all right, but . . .' and it was always in that 'but' that one sensed disapproval.

Rose and I were catching a train from Southampton at six o'clock, and what a very nice man was old Jack, the chauffeur. He got up early to drive us to the station. Fellow travellers stared at us getting out of a lovely car and then entering a third-class carriage.

I'm afraid that Rose didn't enjoy the journey, she was too nervous. I couldn't see why her parents should object to Mr Gerald; after all he wanted to marry their daughter, not set her up in a flat as his mistress. Manchester was a revelation to me; I'd not realised it was so big, or so dirty. The huge Victorian Town Hall was very impressive, but the filth and squalor in some of the streets was appalling. Rose's parents lived in a street slightly better than some we had walked through, inasmuch as most of the houses had proper lace curtains at the windows instead of half-way short net ones, and every doorstep had been whitened with hearthstone. When we reached her home we could see the shadow of her mother through the curtains. Rose had said that her mother wouldn't be waiting on the doorstep for us, it wasn't the done thing, and to pull the lace curtains aside was even worse, it was spying on one's neighbours and only low-class people did that. These working-class social distinctions amazed me; perhaps they were indigenous to the North. Her mother was a tall upright woman with a rather dour expression and I could see that Rose was somewhat in awe of her. The house was a 'two up and down one'; no bathroom, of course, and the lavatory, as usual, in the small yard outside. We were taken into an obviously rarely used sitting-room, and sat down on green plush-covered, straight-backed chairs arranged stiffly around the walls. The over-mantel, draped in green plush, was crowded with china dogs, a matching three-piece set of bright blue china vases and clock, and a photograph in a green velvet frame of Rose as a baby with her ma and pa. He looked a very handsome man and I could see that Rose took after him.

When Rose asked her ma why we couldn't sit in the kitchen, she was told it wasn't the place for guests and, in any case, her father would soon be home from the mill and we'd have dinner there. She turned to me and said that she hoped I liked meat pudding, she didn't hold with all that made-up stuff they ate down in the South. One look at her face and I didn't hold with it either. She added that she was not like some she could name, who never cooked their man a decent meal but sent the kids to the fish and chip shop. And, as for the family that had moved into No 14, she did her step only once a week and it was a disgrace. I reckoned that if I was living in the neighbourhood I'd have given up trying to keep a doorstep white at all.

When her father came in I saw that he'd aged considerably since that photo on the over-mantel. He too was rather dour and silent, and I understood why Rose was nervous. I felt that she had never experienced much overt parental affection; but perhaps that too was indigenous to the North, where working conditions and climate were harder than in the South.

Rose was supposed to tell her father the news while we were having dinner because we'd have to leave before he finished for the day. Her mother asked Rose about Madam; was Madam well and was Madam's husband still as ill-tempered as he used to be, and she'd had a letter from her dear Madam and – suddenly Rose's father broke in angrily:

'For God's sake, enough of your everlasting madaming. The woman's name is Mrs Wardham. She's not God Almighty.'

'Joe Lawton,' answered his wife, 'However you talk in the mill, in this house I'll thank you not to take the name of the Lord in vain.'

Rose remarked timidly that Mrs Wardham was a very nice lady to work for.

'Nice! Don't talk to me about nice. What do those kind of people care about the likes of us. They'd let us starve before they went without a bit of their fat profit. What about your Uncle Fred and his five kids. It's not enough that he's sweating and slaving on his back in the mines every day; now the stinking mine owners want to cut his wages down and do away with the National Wage agreement that the miners had last year. You mark my words, there'll be another strike and it won't be just the miners. Next time the workers will stick together. We've got solidarity. They'll not grind us down for ever.'

Well, after that diatribe, poor Rose hadn't the courage to tell her father that one of the 'grinders' wanted to marry her. I'd have not had the nerve either. After he'd gone back to work and once again we were sitting on those green plush chairs, Rose told her mother the news. At first it was difficult to make her mother understand and, as by this time Rose was almost weeping, I explained it to her as clearly as possible myself.

Her mother sat there looking stunned. Then she said to Rose; 'Never, it can never be. It's not right. What would the likes of us be doing with them upstairs. They're not our kind of people, they don't know the way we live.'

You're right there, I thought. I couldn't see Mr Gerald feeling at home in this street, or being very chummy with Rose's father.

'Besides,' her mother went on, 'whatever shall I say to my madam. How can I tell her such a thing?'

I couldn't see that it mattered in the least what her old Mrs Paine thought about it. And if Mrs Lawton had been my mother, I'd have told her so; but Rose kept silent.

'Your father will never have it, Rose. He's got so bitter lately. They're always having meetings down at the club and he and that Jack Brown and your Uncle John and a few others are always on about a union and a strike, and this time it won't be the same as it was four years ago. They hate the bosses now. No, Rose, your pa had sooner see you struck dead than have one of the rich in his home.'

On the way back to Southampton, Rose was very depressed. I tried to cheer her by saying that her parents, after they'd thought about it, would change their minds, but Rose only moaned that I didn't know her pa. He was as stubborn as a mule and her ma wasn't sympathetic because she thought no good would come of Rose marrying out of her station. Why couldn't Rose be satisfied with a nice hard-working young man like Len, he'd make a good husband.

By the time we got to Redlands, neither of us were very cheerful; and Cook said if that was all a day out did for us we'd as well to be working.

The following week was enlivened for us by the fact that Miss Sarah, the niece who was having her London Season, got engaged.

46

Mr Hall and Mrs Buller wore such benign smiles one would have thought Miss Sarah was their daughter. They said how nice it was for Madam, after all the time she had spent arranging parties and dances, and Madam would be glad to have a rest. Not so glad as *we* would be who'd had all the extra work to do, was the opinion of us under servants; though naturally we didn't voice it.

Miss Sarah hadn't found herself a titled swain from the London Season; nevertheless, her prize came from a good family and had money; so the expenditure on Miss Sarah was well worth it.

So now, the strife being over and the battle won, we could all take things easier and feel that we'd done a good job. I should think that Miss Sarah was even more thankful than us. She was no longer in a market where there were far more sellers than buyers; she'd be able to retire from the competition and contemplate further London Seasons with equanimity, knowing that hers had been a success. How lucky are girls of today, for whom it is no disgrace not to have acquired a husband, and who have been educated to support themselves.

I too would soon be leaving Redlands as Mrs Buller's niece would be coming in three weeks' time. I wouldn't be altogether sorry to leave; I was used to town life and could never settle down in the country. I liked to be amongst crowds of people, and preferred the roar of traffic to bird song.

Mrs Buller was very gracious to me, saying that I was the best kitchenmaid she'd ever had. I expect she thought it was safe to tell me that since I was leaving; if I got a swollen head it wouldn't matter.

All was peace and harmony below stairs at Redlands until one Friday morning, ten days before I was due to finish there.

10

Thursday had been a pleasant day, apart from some discord between young Fred and Mr Burrows. Cook came in to tea looking very amiable; she'd been to a funeral. Cook loved to follow a funeral procession; the slow-moving horses with their black plumes, the carriages full of relatives, the service at the graveside. She always noted whether or not the principal mourners had wept copiously. Nowadays, Cook would need to ride a motor-cycle to be able to follow a funeral.

Violette came in carrying a flowery hat that Madam had just given her. When she tried it on Mr Burrows laughed rudely, and I must admit that although it was a lovely hat it did look rather incongruous perched on top of Violette, with her somewhat dumpy figure and round face.

But young Fred, always kind-hearted, said in what I guessed was bad French, 'Violette, à mon avis, n'importe quoi Beau Brummel ici, votre chapeau est charmant.'

I suppose that Violette knew what he meant, certainly nobody else did. Mr Burrows, who was of the opinion that in the hierarchy of servants, under-gardeners were lower down the scale than valets who were personal servants to gentlemen, couldn't forbear to sneer, though he should have known better than to tangle with young Fred.

'Well, well! Aren't we something with our bit of French. I can see that it won't be long before our Frederic will be tending the gardens at Luxembourg and saying, "Oui, oui Monsieur", instead of all that "Yes, sir, certainly sir", we get at present.'

I had never seen young Fred angry, but for some reason this remark of the valet's seemed to get under his skin; and it made him do something which I'm sure he never meant to do. Pulling a watch from his pocket, young Fred said that his present boss had given him this pocket watch so that at least he'd never be late when he was abroad. That did it as far as the valet was concerned, he was too furious to speak another word. I don't think it was so much that he envied young Fred's acquisition, after all the watch was somewhat shabby. No, what upset Mr Burrows was that the accepted order and tradition of service had been violated. Anything that a madam gave away should go to the ladies' maid, and occasionally the head housemaid, and anything that one's gentleman disposed of should go first to the valet and then to the butler. But I think that Mr Wardham disliked indoor servants as much as he seemed to dislike his own family. And so, having nobody to talk to indoors, he made a confidante of young Fred who, for a working-class man, was better educated than most.

Friday was a catastrophic day. Well, to be honest, Mary, Doris and I thought it an exciting day, the like of which we'd never seen before and were not likely to see again. The trouble started while Mr Wardham was having breakfast and reading his letters. Suddenly, the breakfast-room bell started ringing; it rang and it rang and, when Mr Hall hurried to answer it, he was told by a furious Mr Wardham to fetch Mr Gerald down immediately. What took place then we learnt only gradually. First from the butler and valet, who were hovering in the hall listening to the loud and angry altercations between Mr Wardham and Gerald. Later on we heard it from Rose herself.

It transpired that Mr Wardham had received a letter from Rose's father. After she had told her mother about Gerald, knowing that the father would be enraged, her mother had let a day or so elapse before telling him. The following evening, Rose's father had written a long and bitter letter to Mr Wardham, to the effect that no daughter of his was going to marry into a class of idle rich who lived off the blood and sweat of the poor. Some months later, Rose showed this letter to Mary and me. Her father had certainly poured out old rancours and grievances; no doubt they'd been smouldering over the years. It was as though all the hunger and hardships he'd suffered in his youth had crystallised into the shape of Mr Wardham and his son.

He had written that as one of ten children, he'd gone into the mill at ten years old and worked in his bare feet from seven o'clock in the morning until eight o'clock at night; and anybody who wasted even a minute talking to another worker was fined or got the sack. And the stinking rich mill owner would drive up to the mill in his carriage and pair and the coachman would open the door for him as though he was bloody royalty. When he came into the mill everybody had to be working full out or they'd get sacked; the mill owner didn't care who starved or died from overwork so long as he could live in a big house with servants to wait on him. But the time was coming when the workers would rise up and unite against bosses who ground down the workers.

There was more in the same vein but, as Rose said, what had it got to do with her and Gerald. He was different from his father as shown by the fact that he wouldn't let Mr Burrows valet him.

But on the morning of the row between Mr Wardham and his son, Rose couldn't speak so calmly about the affair; in fact she was weeping most of the day. When Madam came downstairs, looking very upset, she said that she wanted to speak to Rose privately in our servants' hall. They were there over half-an-hour, and when Mrs Wardham came out she told the butler that Rose wasn't to wait at table, for that day at least. And she told all of us that she hoped we wouldn't discuss the matter – what a forlorn hope – and in particular the upper servants were not to reprimand Rose in any way. I thought how kind she was to say that and how well she understood servants; because most assuredly the upper servants would have attacked Rose. As it was, all they could do was to look hostile. Mrs Buller wasn't too bad, though when she heard Doris and me whispering in the scullery she came in and caustically told us not to worry, such an astonishing event, in the nature of things, could never happen to us. Doris merely giggled but I was secretly annoyed, for, although I hadn't the attractions of Rose, I was better looking than Doris. The butler came into the kitchen to complain to Cook about having to do the waiting at table on his own and he'd like to know what was going to happen after that day. Cook commiserated with him, saying that the late, loved and lamented Mr Buller – one of nature's gentleman – would turn in his grave to hear of such a thing. The late Mr Buller had been highly respected by his employers because he always knew his place; he'd never at any time become familiar.

When the day was over and we went to bed, none of us took any notice of Cook's admonishment that we were not to gossip half the night. With the under servants Rose became more cheerful, though evasive about any future plans. It was obvious to us that already she was feeling a 'somebody' and not just Rose, a parlourmaid. We didn't blame her for it, we'd all have felt the same in the circumstances – well, perhaps Doris wouldn't; any contact with them above stairs reduced her to a mute figure. Mary and I freely gave Rose the benefit of our advice, though as we'd never been in a similar situation our advice wasn't worth much. We told her not to be persuaded to give up Gerald, such a golden opportunity might never present itself again, and what was the point of throwing away her youth and beauty on that Len her Mum wanted her to marry. If she married him, she'd be living in a 'two up and downer', have half-a-dozen kids and in no time at all lose her looks and figure. We went on talking until Cook knocked on our door and told us to go to sleep. When Mary and I woke the next morning the third bed was empty and Rose had gone. There was a note on the bed saying that she'd left with Gerald and would write to us later on.

Mary and I, though sorry that we hadn't been able to say goodbye to Rose, were nevertheless gratified to be the bearers of such portentous news, and great was the consternation of the upper servants when they heard. The butler all but directly accused Mary and me of knowing that Rose was departing in the night, but we hadn't known that she was going. Sometime during the day Rose must have packed her small suitcase – she'd left most of her clothes in the wardrobe – hidden it under the bed and crept out so silently that we'd heard no noise at all. Madam was shown the note that Rose had left and told Cook that she hoped all was well with Rose.

Naturally, it was the one and only topic of conversation at dinner. Mr Hall seemed to be particularly incensed, as though Rose had done him a personal injury. Sitting at one end of the table, looking like a modern Mr Bumble, he started to say, very pompously, 'In all my years in service, man and boy', when young Fred interrupted, 'Boy and man'.

'What d'you mean?'

'You can't say, "man and boy",' young Fred explained, 'it's the wrong way round.'

Ignoring this, beyond glaring at the interrupter, Mr Hall went on to say that, man and boy, he'd never known the like. It was all owing to Gerald being in Rhodesia and coming back with all those mad ideas that white people shouldn't be servants. And what, Mr Hall demanded to known, would happen to all of us; what other work could we do? Mark his words, Rose would live to regret it.

'I think that it will be Mr Gerald who will regret it,' said young Fred.

'Ah!' sneered Mr Burrows, 'You would say that, you were sweet on Rose yourself.'

'Sweet on Rose, I never was, I always thought that apart from being extremely pretty, there was nothing to her. She'd no conversation, never read a book, took no interest in politics or the world around her. I reckon that unless she gets herself an education, learns to speak well, can discuss the theatre and the arts, Mr Gerald will get bored with just gazing at a pretty face.'

Hearing this, Mary and I, not having pretty faces, endeavoured to appear as intelligent as possible, while Doris looking at us just giggled; then, receiving a severe look and a rebuke from Mr Hall, she burst into tears.

Mrs Buller who, although she sometimes reprimanded poor Doris, never allowed anybody else to do so, gave the butler a hard look and said, 'Mr Hall, I'll thank you not to exceed your obligations by assuming responsibility for my staff – in the absence of your own.'

That just about did it. Mr Burrows tittered and young Fred burst out laughing – old Fred being deaf hadn't heard a word. Mr Hall slowly rose from the table, the very embodiment of outraged dignity – though being fat and balding the effect wasn't all that impressive – and left the room. In the normal way, Mrs Buller wouldn't have made such a sarcastic remark; but for the time being the whole discipline of below stairs was suspended. Events were too much out of this world. Rose and Gerald gone, and Mr Wardham raging and venting his spite and anger on poor Madam and Miss Helen. Why, according to Mr Hall, the Master had turned on Miss Helen and said that nobody was likely to run away with her in the night.

I wasn't sorry when my time was up and I left Redlands. Mrs Wardham, kind as ever, gave me an extra £5, and Cook even kissed me goodbye. Mary too would soon be leaving to become a house-maid, she reckoned she'd done her time as an 'under'.

11

My first place as a cook was in Kensington, and it was certainly a contrast to working at Redlands. For one thing, there were only three servants; cook, housemaid and parlourmaid. And for another, my employer, a Lady Gibbons, was a very different type of person from Mrs Wardham. Lady Gibbons was harsh and tyrannical; so much so that there was a constant procession of housemaids and parlourmaids who found her impossible to work for. As a cook, I saw her only in the mornings when she came down to give the orders for the day. I was dismayed to find that I had to cook on a kitchen range. Many houses, especially in London, were doing away with these coal-consuming objects and using gas stoves for the cooking and coke boilers for a constant supply of hot water. I know that some people can cook to perfection on a kitchen range, but I never could. Either it would be roaring like a furnace, or not hot enough. There was a small gas stove but it was only allowed to be used to boil kettles for early morning tea and for filling the hot-water bottles at night. Such was Lady Gibbons's distrust of servants that she seemed to have developed a sixth sense about them. If I'd let the fire get low and used that gas stove, sure enough she'd come to the top of the basement stairs and call down, 'Cook, can I smell gas?' I'd make out that a tap had inadvertently got turned on.

Mind you, Lady Gibbons had plenty to put up with from me for I was by no means a good cook. I thought I could cook when I got the job, but I found that the amount I knew as a kitchenmaid was somewhat inadequate when it came to doing everything. The first dish I came a cropper over was a very simple dish; you wouldn't have thought that I could go wrong making it – well, I wouldn't have if Lady Gibbons had had it made the way I'd seen cooks make it. The dish was a bread-and-butter pudding. I'd always seen cooks make it with nice thin slices of bread and butter, interspersed with currants and sugar, and a custard made with eggs poured over before baking the dish. But the first one I made for Lady Gibbons was on a Monday night, using all the crusts that had accumulated through the week, with a dab of margarine on, and a custard made with custard powder poured over before baking. I'd never made custard with powder before but, if I'd had the sense to realise that I shouldn't have let it thicken before pouring it over the chunks of bread, it wouldn't have been so bad. As it was, the thick custard never penetrated through the bread. Still, I can't see that it was my fault and, if they suffered above stairs with my cooking, our life was pretty grim. The attic bedroom I shared with the parlourmaid was barely furnished; a cupboard each for our clothes, two wooden chairs, a strip of matting on the linoleum and one washstand for the two of us. There was no bathroom for the servants, only one of those old hip-baths.

The new parlourmaid, named Olive, was a young girl of fifteen, though how she could be a fully-fledged parlourmaid at that age I couldn't see, until I discovered that Lady Gibbons, despairing of getting an experienced parlourmaid, had decided to train a young girl. Olive came from a somewhat remote little village; I expect Lady Gibbons thought a country girl would be more malleable than a girl used to town life. Olive had a very sweet and amiable nature, and she was attractive too. It seemed to be my fate to be friendly with girls so much better-looking than me.

About three weeks after leaving Redlands, Mary sent me a letter she'd had from Rose. The news was that she and Gerald were not yet married – I wondered if they were living in sin – but Gerald had been to Manchester to see Rose's father. He'd made such a good impression on him that now her father had withdrawn his strong objections to the marriage, and Rose and Gerald would be married in two weeks' time. They were to have a registry office marriage and Rose was so sorry that she couldn't invite Mary and Margaret, but Gerald wanted to have a quiet wedding.

I bet he does too, I thought. The last thing he's likely to want is a reminder of his wife's origins. I wondered what he'd thought of the 'two up and downer' that was Rose's home. If he drove up in his bright red car, I bet the neighbours had an eyeful. I wouldn't have minded betting that Rose's ma had asked the street to make their doorsteps especially white for the occasion. She was the kind of woman who'd have the nerve to ask it.

I told Olive about the good fortune of the under-parlourmaid I knew, and Olive, being a dreamy girl and prone to romantic fancies, immediately began to create an imaginary situation whereby the same thing happened to her – and I will say this: Olive had a much better voice than Rose. But even Olive's vivid imagination couldn't romanticise Lady Gibbons's son. He was sandy-haired with a receding chin, about five foot nothing, and he took about as much notice of servants as he did of a beetle beneath his feet.

Now that we had a parlourmaid we were without a housemaid, Jessica having left two or three weeks after I arrived. I did think of writing to Mary to suggest she come, but then realised that I wouldn't want to inflict Lady Gibbons on a friend. In any case I'd have been too late as Mary had already agreed to be a single-handed housemaid with a family in Chelsea.

She came to see me on her first free afternoon bringing a female whom she introduced as her cousin, Zena. This cousin was a revelation to Olive and me. Not only was she married, but she was still working. It was almost unheard of for a woman to go out to work when she had a husband, but Zena was smart and sophisticated. Her make-up was perfect inasmuch as one could tell that she had used it, but it made an harmonious whole instead of the clown effect that Mary and I sometimes achieved. I could see that Mary had already gained in looks from her cousin's ministrations and I naturally resolved to find out how it was done. Zena worked in a fashion house, which I suppose was the reason she was so well-dressed, and she certainly looked far younger than her age of forty-five years. Mary had only just found out that she had this cousin, and it was apparent that she felt a certain pride in having a relation so different from us. Zena's husband worked for a pharmaceutical firm and travelled a lot so, she told us, she had a free life. What she did with this freedom wasn't discussed then, except that Zena said she spent a lot of time soaking herself in a highly-scented bath – that was where she got her ideas for designing her clothes – and it passed the time while Brian was away. It seemed a peculiar way of passing the time and, as I said to Olive later on, if Zena was with us in Kensington, she'd get very few ideas sitting in our bath-tub with a handful of soda in the water. Nevertheless, she brought a bit of life into our servants' hall with her tales about the vagaries of customers who were convinced that they could wear a dress that was obviously two sizes too small.

Mary said she hadn't been sorry to get away from Redlands. The discord in the family above stairs had repercussions on the servants below; the butler and valet were always bickering and Cook seemed snappish with everybody. Her new place in Chelsea wasn't bad, though her Madam was nothing like so kind as Mrs Wardham – nor was mine either, not by a long shot. The staff consisted of Mary, a butler and a cook; and an odd-job man, Alf, for cleaning the steps, boots and knives and getting in the coal for the range. Alf, who was about thirty-five and unmarried, did this job every morning in addition to his own work with a firm of window-cleaners; obviously an early case of moonlighting.

I rather envied Mary's job where there were two men around. It was not that one necessarily wanted to feel romantic about the male servants, but just nice to have some contact with the opposite sex.

Mary had brought a letter with her from Rose inviting us to tea, but not on a Sunday as Gerald refused to have visitors then. He liked

Sundays to be kept free so that he and Rose could be alone in their own little house in Hampstead. How very sweet of him, we thought, and wondered how long that would last. Mary and I agreed that in all probability the reason we were invited on a weekday was because Gerald wouldn't be at home to see us. And so it proved.

When Mary and I saw the size of the 'little' house in Hampstead, we both felt that Rose could no longer be one of us. The house was double-fronted, large and solid. It even had a trades-mans entrance, and Mary and I stood on the pavement debating whether we should use it – not seriously of course. We rang the bell and were taken aback when the door was opened by a stern-faced, middle-aged woman wearing a black dress and a frilly white apron. She informed us that Mrs Wardham would be down in a few minutes and showed us into what we supposed was the drawing-room.

When she'd gone, Mary and I looked at each other and, with difficulty, suppressed our laughter. Mary, who was quite a good mimic, said, 'Sit down, girl. Mrs Wardham will shortly appear to interview you. I hope that your references are excellent as Mrs Wardham couldn't possibly employ you otherwise. Mrs Wardham's servants have always come from the best families.' We then giggled madly but I was nevertheless rather annoyed. Why couldn't Rose have welcomed us in? She knew what time we were arriving.

When Rose eventually arrived, we saw a transformation from the Rose that we'd known. She was wearing a blue silk dress that was obviously expensive, as were the black patent shoes, pearl necklace and diamond ring, not to mention the elaborately-waved hair. I didn't know about Mary, but I felt like a poor relation. Fortunately, when she spoke, it was still the same Rose with the same excruciating accent, now overlaid by falsely genteel tones.

'Lovely to see you again, Mary and Margaret. How nice you both look. Mrs Brookes will be bringing in the tea in a few minutes. She's my housekeeper, you know. Gerald says that I can't possibly look after this house on my own.'

What rubbish, 'housekeeper'! It was just an euphemism for a general servant. How could she possibly be a housekeeper when she was the only maid employed. Mary and I were embarrassed at sitting there doing nothing while Mrs Brookes brought in a heavy tea-tray. Mary, with more curiosity than tact, asked Rose how Gerald could afford all this; the large house, expensively furnished, and the servant. Wasn't Gerald dependent on his father?

'Of course he isn't,' exclaimed Rose, somewhat indignantly, 'he has money of his own. Mrs Wardham bought this house for us as a wedding present. Besides, Gerald's gone into partnership with a man in the City and he's doing ever so well. His partner's ever so nice; we went to his house to dinner the other evening, he's got a lovely place near Ascot and his wife's ever so nice.'

I inwardly winced at all these 'ever so nice's' and wondered how Gerald managed; he probably tried to keep his wife's conversation to a minimum.

On the way back, Mary and I agreed that our visit to Rose hadn't really been a success. Now that she was married to Gerald, she didn't want to talk about Redlands or the Wardhams. Mary and I had found ourselves with very little to say after we'd finished talking about our new Madams – or My-lady, as it was in my case. For all the fine establishment and servant too, Rose's life seemed singularly dull. She'd been nowhere and done nothing.

'I don't know about you, Margaret,' said Mary, 'but I expected something better than that. Two cups of weak tea, such soppy little sandwiches that six of them only made a mouthful, and one slice of cake. All that bus fare to Hampstead for such a stingy tea.'

'Yes, it wasn't exactly a gargantuan feast, Mary. And you might as well have saved your breath instead of dropping all those hints about sherry and the boyfriend who brought you two glasses of the stuff in a pub. Not a whiff of the sherry bottle did we get.'

'Did you notice how Rose kept watching the clock towards the end? I'm sure she was getting in a state in case that precious Gerald came back and we were still there. Wouldn't that have ruined his day, to find two of his wife's low-class friends sitting in his drawing-room. And d'you remember, Margaret, him saying there shouldn't be white servants? And now he employs a housekeeper. What a hypocrite! I don't envy Rose.'

That was a lie if ever there was one. We both envied Rose and both felt that we'd make a better job of being Gerald's wife than she would. But having by this time got over our rancour at the luke-warm reception, we went to Lyons Corner House for a good feed and the faint hope of picking-up two young men – or even one between us if two were not available. In the event, the only unattached males were the men in the band. I told Mary not to bother with them. Although it wasn't the same band as when I was last there with Gladys, a friend of mine, they were probably no better. Gladys and I, by means of passing notes, had managed to make a date with two of the bandsmen; but we'd found that although they were real-looking men in uniform, when they were out of it and wearing flashy pin-striped suits, they were two of the weediest specimens of manhood one could imagine. And for a tenpenny seat in the pictures and a fourpenny ice-cream, the fellow I was with thought he was entitled to the works. Exasperated, I used 'urgent need' as my excuse, and I left him waiting for me outside a ladies lavatory and departed by a different door. Comparing our evening, Gladys and I agreed that men were pretty awful, but what could we do? We wanted to get married not just to get out of domestic service, but because to be a spinster was looked upon almost with contempt as indicating a woman who lacked what it takes.

Mary and I arranged to meet on the following Sunday, her next free afternoon and evening. I, as a cook, was free every Sunday after the midday meal. I wondered if I would survive until the next Sunday as on Friday there was to be a dinner party. Only five people had been invited, making eight in all, so it wasn't to be like the dinner parties at Redlands. But Mrs Buller had had Doris and me to help her, while I was cooking single-handed.

Lady Gibbons had at last managed to get a housemaid, who had been ordered – not asked – to help Olive with the waiting at table. It wasn't really a housemaid's job to do this, but in domestic service there was no rigid demarcation line. In any case Amy, the housemaid, was in no position to refuse. At her age it wasn't so easy to get work, and as she had no relatives it meant getting a furnished room every time she lost a job. Considering it was my first attempt at cooking a dinner for eight people, I reckon I did very well. Fortunately, I knew that I could use the gas stove with impunity; Lady Gibbons would never have had the nerve to call down on such an important occasion. There were four courses: clear soup – a fairly easy but tedious job; fried fillets of sole with tartare sauce; lamb cutlets served on a bed of mashed and creamed potatoes, with stuffed baked tomatoes and creamed spinach. I tried to get away with just chopping the spinach but I could see it didn't look right so I had to rub the lot through a wire sieve. The last course was a cold lemon soufflé, which I managed to turn out of the mould without breaking the shape. Poor Amy then got flustered and broke the glass dish, but fortunately for me they'd eaten the soufflé by then. Olive was given a 6/- (about 30p now) tip which she generously shared out – it wasn't to be sneezed at. I bought two pairs of artificial silk stockings with my share. That was all we did get, Lady Gibbons never even said thank you.

When I met Mary on the Sunday, she said that we'd been invited to a party at her Aunt Ellie's. This was the aunt who'd been a waitress and married a wealthy man – one of her regular customers. Mary and I were quite impressed with her aunt's new house, though when we were introduced to her husband, we thought he looked considerably older than her aunt had made him out to be. Perhaps travelling abroad with Aunt Ellie had aged him. I was cottoned on to by a young man called Steve, one of the young waiters where Aunt Ellie had worked. When I asked him what he did in his spare time, he said his hobby was playing the ivories. I thought that meant he played the piano, but no; he meant he was a dominoes champion. What a game to be a champion of! I used to play dominoes with my children and wondered why the youngest was always getting the double six, until I discovered that he'd made a faint mark on the back of it. Steve's dominoes were white with black spots, instead of the more usual black set with white spots. But it never works out to have anything to do with a man who has a hobby. When first he's enamoured of you, *you* are his hobby; but after a few weeks, when the impact of your charms has faded, he thinks again of his first love – in Steve's case, dominoes. I went out with him for a few weeks and he took me later on to have tea with his parents. His mother was very friendly – as she'd three other children, perhaps she was keen to get Steve off her hands. His father said, 'How do' and not much more; but I didn't mind that, my father too was a quiet man. Steve's grandmother lived with them, an ebullient and garrulous old dear, and the tea-time was enlivened by old gran giving a monologue on Bert her long departed husband.

'I tell you, Maggie' – 'I'm called Margaret', I murmured, but she took no notice – 'our old panel doctor said he'd never in his life seen a case like my Bert's. He was just eaten away, eaten away he was, like those ants in the desert ate the man those Arabs buried in the sand in that film we saw last week.'

As an accompaniment to the buttered scones it wasn't what I would have chosen, but all the others went on munching; I suppose they'd heard it many times. Gran hadn't finished:

'My Bert broke his leg, Maggie, and gangrene set in all because my Bert wouldn't let them take his leg off. "No", said my Bert, "I came into this world with two legs and I'm going to leave it the same way." Suffered awful he did, and the gangrene crept higher and higher. But my Bert wouldn't have his leg off.'

Steve did make a half-hearted attempt to stop gran's gory reminiscences, but obviously nobody else seemed to mind. Anyway, my romance with him soon finished for he started taking me into the pub where he used to play dominoes and, in no time at all, there he was playing them again. I very soon got bored sitting around sipping an occasional port, and no conversation. I could see that Steve would never be a permanent boyfriend. There is some prestige attached to being a grass widow for golf or cricket; but dominoes, never.

Mary's aunt had introduced her to 'such a nice boy'; but the nice boy was out of work, having lost three jobs in as many months. For two weeks Mary paid when they went out, but when that Maurice showed no sign of getting a job Mary said goodbye. Her cousin had lent us the recently published *Gentlemen Prefer Blondes* and, as Mary said, one could see that a mother was no longer a girl's best friend, it was diamonds. But sadly her hopes of getting any were so remote as to be practically non-existent.

Mary, ever philosophical, said what did boyfriends matter when we'd got our health and strength, but I couldn't agree with her. If we never managed to get a permanent male while we had our health and strength, it was for certain we wouldn't when we were old and feeble, and then we wouldn't be able to work either.

I certainly needed to be healthy for when I had been in the basement four months, Lady Gibbons and Sir Walter decided to go to Yorkshire for two months while the son was abroad. She gave Amy notice, found a place for Olive – I'd never have gone to any place Lady Gibbons recommended – and put me on board wage, fifteen shillings a week. I went home for two weeks but for the other six I had to clean the house all on my own. I wasn't a bit nervous then of being alone in a large house, though I would be now. Mary, Olive and Gladys came round when they were free, though they had to bring food; my fifteen shillings wasn't enough to feed more than one and Lady Gibbons had locked up all the stores.

Mary and I had heard nothing from Rose since we'd seen her four months ago, but one morning I got a letter saying that she was longing to see us. Could we come on Wednesday, she asked, as Gerald would be away for the night. She simply must talk to somebody.

12

This time, when we arrived at 'Melrose', we braced ourselves in anticipation of facing the redoubtable housekeeper, Mrs Brookes, only to find, when the door opened a young maid about fifteen years old. Rose came rushing out of the drawing-room to greet us, saying that she was so pleased to see us and hoped we wouldn't need to rush away.

'What's happened to your Mrs Brookes, then?' asked Mary.

'Oh, I had to get rid of her. The way that woman went on, you'd have thought she was mistress of this house. And she was always spying on me. I couldn't stand it.'

Why should Rose imagine that Mrs Brookes was spying on her? What was there to discover that could be detrimental? I felt sure that Rose was living a perfectly respectable life in her little Hampstead home. I did notice that she seemed to be in a rather nervous state, babbling away without pausing for breath. I couldn't make out half of what she said but I understood her final words, would we like a drink. Mary had the gall to remark on our way back that if Rose had spoken in Hindustani, I'd have still grasped the words about having a drink. Anyway, by the time that we'd knocked back a couple of gin-and-its, Rose seemed more like the old Rose that we'd known below stairs. How different it was from our previous visit when she'd not said a word against Gerald, nor would listen to any adverse comment from us. Now her grievances poured out like a cataract. She hated living in this house, it was too big. She was lonely, there were no next-door neighbours like her mother had, in Hampstead – I should think not, I interrupted. She had nothing to do all day and Gerald never came home before six o'clock, and even then he was shut in his study working. And when she complained he said, very sarcastically, that although she was no longer a parlour-maid, there was a full-time job ready to hand in getting herself an education. She could make a start by reading some proper books instead of trashy romances and magazines; take herself off to museums and art galleries where she'd learn that life didn't start in the slums of Manchester. And, she might usefully take some elocution lessons to eradicate the excruciating accent. Here Rose started to weep and Mary and I looked at each other in amazement. Love's young dream had certainly faded. Through her tears, Rose said that the first two or three times they'd quarrelled Gerald had been so loving afterwards, saying he hadn't meant it and he loved her so much and was there anything she would like. But now he was either silent or sarcastic, saying that the reason they had no social life was because every time she opened her mouth she let him down. Why couldn't she try to be like Sheila, his partner's wife. Look at the way she gave little dinner parties and always had plenty to say. People liked to be invited to Ronald and Sheila's home, but none of his friends wanted to come to them, with Rose sitting like a blockhead at the table.

After spilling all this out, Rose gradually became more cheerful and eventually suggested that we go into the kitchen and have something to eat and a bottle of wine; she'd told Alice to take the evening off. Rose may have sat like a blockhead with her husband's friends, but she had plenty to say to Mary and me.

'You know, it all started when Mrs Stone came.'

'Who's Mrs Stone, then?'

'She's the woman who comes three mornings a week to do the rough work. I found out that she used to live in Salford so it's only natural that I liked to talk to her, me coming from so near to her home. When Gerald's home on a Saturday, he don't like me talking to her in what he says is a familiar manner. He says that I don't belong to that kind of life any longer and that I'll never learn to speak properly if I keep talking to Mrs Stone. But why should I be different? Just because Gerald's been to a public school and can talk in that posh voice. He knew what I was when he fell in love and we got married. Why should he want me to change? He hasn't got the right, has he?'

Rose didn't really want any reasoned answers from us, all she wanted was sympathy and the assurance that she was not to blame. But I felt Gerald had some justification for his complaints. He was providing Rose with a fairly luxurious home, lovely clothes and somebody to do the work. He was entitled to something in return. I wondered if she would accept any constructive criticism.

'Why don't you take elocution lessons, Rose? It might be quite fun, and at least it would give you something to do and get you out of the house.'

'Margaret, how can I go home and start talking in a la-di-da voice. Ma and Pa wouldn't like it. They'd say that I was showing them up in front of the neighbours. Down our street they stick together, they don't like the bosses.'

I wanted to say the obvious: she didn't live in that street now and, if all she wanted was a life the same as her parents had, she'd have been better off if she'd married Len. But saying that wouldn't have helped Rose. So I said, trying to make my voice sound light and casual, 'I love going to museums and art galleries, Rose, but I never have anybody to go with. Why don't you come with me? I'm free any afternoon while Lady Gibbons is away.'

I half expected Rose to be as derisive about the proposition as Mary would have been. But instead of an emphatic negative, she wondered if she would be interested – and it would please Gerald – and yes she would come with me but not to look at paintings; she just couldn't see why people wanted to gaze at dreary old pictures of horses and battles and kings and queens. Why, her aunt Gertie painted pictures of things like flowers and gardens and they were ever so pretty. Much as I liked Rose, I thought yet again how utterly inane was her conversation. I remembered young Fred's remark that it was Gerald he felt sorry for, married to Rose.

On the journey back from Hampstead, Mary asked why on earth I'd offered to take Rose to a museum.

'Margaret, she'll be even more bored than I was. Can you imagine her going into raptures over some old Roman relics, or exclaiming about the beauty of the statues. I bet you, by the time Rose has been in a museum for half-an-hour, she'll suggest going for a cup of tea in Lyons. I know Rose better than you do, Margaret. She'll not change. For all her fine house and clothes and a husband from upstairs, in the long run she'd be happier with that Len. Her heart's with them at the mill, not in the mansion. You mark my words, that marriage won't last.'

Remembering Mary's gloomy words about the impossibility of educating Rose, I felt like a martyr as I waited for her outside the British Museum, and she certainly had the look of one as we entered. I made straight for my favourite gallery to show Rose the ancient Greek sculptures. I loved them, and in spite of the DO NOT TOUCH notices I could never forbear to lightly feel the stone and marvel anew; that such beauty as this existed so many centuries ago!

If I had any idea or hope that Rose would share my enthusiasm, I was quickly disillusioned. She gazed at the wonderful relics of an ancient civilisation with lack-lustre eyes and, after a few minutes, said in a plaintive voice, 'But it's all so dead, Margaret. Isn't there anything that moves?'

I answered, more sharply than I meant to, that the place was a museum, not a fairground. We removed ourselves to a gallery where were displayed the more modern artefacts – well, modern in comparison to Greek – beautiful vases, figurines and intricate ornaments. But all Rose could say was that they were 'just things'. I suppose if one was incapable of visualising the lives of people who actually lived with, and used these lovely objects, then they *were* 'just things'.

So, as Mary had prophesied, I saw that it was a waste of time staying any longer in the British Museum and we went to Lyons for a cup of tea. While we were there Rose said that she'd love to have an evening out; couldn't we go to the Hammersmith Palais, where she could dance with ordinary young men and not be expected to carry on a conversation at the same time. She could telephone Gerald's office to say that she was spending the evening with me; she could call him from my place, we'd have to go back there for me to change. I hastily told Rose that she couldn't use Lady Gibbons' telephone, I'd be in trouble if she was charged for a call while she was in Yorkshire. The telephone in the kitchen was only for calling tradesmen who were late with orders or had delivered the wrong thing.

Rose telephoned her husband from a callbox, and when I asked if he'd minded her being out for the evening Rose said, rather sadly, 'No, he didn't mind at all. He said he'd be late home as he had to meet a client, and I was to have a nice evening. He's probably glad to be without me.'

When Rose saw below stairs at Lady Gibbons', the dark basement, the cheerless servants' hall, all so drab and dreary a contrast to our good quarters at Redlands, and then saw my equally spartan bedroom, she exclaimed, 'However can you live here, Margaret? I think it's all horrible, nothing nice for the servants at all. Whatever made you take this place?'

I was tempted to reply, 'Because I couldn't find anybody eager to transport me to a life of ease and comfort in Hampstead', but thought such an answer would not be very tactful. All the time I was changing Rose kept up a lamentation about her life; the loneliness, the inexperience of the present maid, the airs and graces of the departed Mrs Brookes and the unkindness of Gerald complaining that Rose wasn't 'social'.

I became rather irritated listening to her complaints. After all, she'd chosen her life and, with a bit of determination and ambition, she could live and cope in Gerald's world. Interrupting her monologue, I quoted from Longfellow:

'Tell me not, in mournful numbers,
Life is but an empty dream!
For the soul is dead that slumbers,
And things are not what they seem.'

But apart from Rose saying, 'Oh, Margaret, I wish I was as clever as you', my attempts to cheer her made no impression. I felt her mournful mood hardly presaged a lively evening at the Palais, but I was wrong. Of course, a girl as pretty as Rose never became a wallflower at a dance; but on this occasion even I did well – which gave me enough confidence to skim around the dance floor as though I weighed seven stone instead of nearer eleven. I even managed to make a date with a quite presentable looking young man for the Saturday night dance. Rose put rather a damper on this achievement by saying she wouldn't have anything to do with a young man who met you inside a dance-hall – so that he didn't have to pay your entrance fee. But then Rose always had more chances than I'd had. She could have left the Palais with the choice of any one of half-a-dozen young men, but Rose would never do such a thing now that she was married. We got a taxi and she insisted on its taking me back before going on to Hampstead. I lent Rose my copy of A. S. M. Hutchinson's, *If Winter Comes*. I spent far too much of my wages on books – and told her it was a wonderful story. Gerald would be pleased to see her reading it instead of *Hearts Aflame*. Rose went back to Hampstead looking happier than when we'd met outside the Museum, and I'd had a good evening too. I wasn't to know then that when I turned up at the Palais on Saturday, there wouldn't be a sign of the presentable conquest I thought I'd made.

13

Naturally, I had to tell Mary about the outcome of the British Museum episode; she nobly refrained from saying, 'I told you so'. We were queueing up to see Rudolph Valentino in *The Four Horsemen of the Apocalypse* and Mary was quite right in saying that an afternoon at the pictures would be far more in Rose's line than a cultural afternoon. She reckoned the marriage might last another year and then Gerald would want a divorce. I felt sure that Rose, with her innate respectability, and influenced by the rigid and narrow religious views of her mother would never consider divorcing Gerald, whatever evidence he gave her. And, as the only ground for it was adultery, Gerald would never be able to divorce Rose.

Anyway, as Lady Gibbons had returned from Yorkshire, I had far less time to think about Rose and her matrimonial problems. Lady Gibbons had brought back a sixteen-year-old girl from the remote village where they'd stayed; she was to be the housemaid and, as Lady Gibbons had her name down at three registry offices, she hoped soon to have a parlourmaid as well. The house was subjected to a thorough inspection, on Lady Gibbons's return. She needed to be satisifed that the two month's board wages she'd paid me, in addition to my monthly wage, had been worth the outlay. Actually I worked for her for only another four months before I decided to give in my notice. This was partly owing to the redcurrant jelly that I was expected to make. At that time I'd never in my life made jam, let alone jelly. I couldn't get the stuff to set. I kept boiling it but still it was runny, so at last, in desperation I melted some sheets of gelatine in the redcurrants. After that it set so hard that when I dropped one lot on the floor it bounced. As the redcurrant jelly made by some previous cook was nearly all gone, I thought it would be better if I wasn't there when my concoction was opened.

Mary's Aunt Elly asked why I didn't get out of domestic service, I could easily get a job as a waitress in a Lyons teashop. I'd have a livelier time and see more people. But somehow I couldn't fancy myself as a Nippy and the opportunity of falling into the arms of a wealthy widower – as Aunt Elly had done – was too remote even to contemplate. Besides, if I became a waitress I'd have to choose between living at home or in a furnished room; neither prospect appealed to me. In any case I'd decided to do temporary work as a cook; I wouldn't stay long in any one place and I'd get a lot of experience. The first place I took was a disaster; not so the second. I was there because their cook was ill, not because they couldn't get one. I was actually allowed to go into the library and borrow any books I wanted to read. To be able to do this was, to me, like an open sesame to Ali Baba's cave. There were literally hundreds of books in huge bookcases lining the four walls. Not only the classics – I read those too – but modern books such as Aldous Huxley's *Antic Hay* and *Chrome Yellow*; authors like William Locke and Ethel M. Dell. When, after three months, their own cook was well enough to start work, I was certainly sorry to leave.

I hadn't seen either Rose or Mary for about six weeks. Where Mary was concerned it was because she'd met such a gentlemanly young man whom she hoped would become a 'permanent', and therefore all her free time had to be spent with him. Actually, I was in rather an invidious position. It was through me that Mary had met her Harold, who at that time was the boyfriend of Gladys's. Gladys wanted me to meet this Harold, so one Sunday afternoon, taking Mary with me, we went to Hyde Park where we'd arranged to meet. We stood by Speakers' Corner and I remember that there was a fat, red-faced man there, ranting on about the 'rights of the common man'. Mary whispered to me that he looked about as common as could be so presumably he was speaking from a personal viewpoint.

'My name's Bill Robinson', he bawled, 'and I fought in the war to make this a land fit for heroes. And what have I got for it? What have any of us old soldiers got for it? A putty medal and goodbye, we don't want to know you until the next bloody war. Get yourself a job or starve on the dole. The bloody government don't care a damn about the likes of us working class people. But the day will come, my friends –'

Here he'd been stopped by another bawling voice, 'I ain't no bloody friend of yours Bill Robinson or whatever you call yourself, and by the looks of you, you ain't starving neither.'

Seeing that the barracker was only a weedy little man, the speaker told him to shut his bloody gob or he'd do it for him. Amid the general laughter, we met Gladys and her 'gentleman friend'. I took an instant dislike to him as his pallid limp hand shook mine. Later on, in a teashop, holding his cup with the little finger outstretched, this Harold told Mary and me that he was head assistant in a men's outfitters. I discovered that there were only two assistants so he wasn't head of much. He spoke in an artificially refined voice about his father, a clerk; his sister, a teacher; his brother, a dental mechanic; until I felt like asking what were we supposed to be doing, playing 'happy families?' I could see however, that Mary was taken with him as we listened to a monologue about his life behind the counter. Still, give him his due, he offered to take us dancing. I could see from the look on Gladys's face, that she had no wish to be lumbered with us two for the entire evening, so I said that Mary and I were going to the pictures. Mary protested that we could go to the pictures any time, she much preferred to dance. Besides, she'd just learnt how to do the Charleston and what a marvellous dance it was. Vapid Harold trotted out the joke that was going the rounds – we'd all heard it before – that the Charleston was invented by a girl trying to get a bent penny in the lavatory lock. We all went dancing and the evening was ruined for Gladys because, in no time at all, Mary was showing Harold how to do the Charleston and Gladys and I had to dance with each other. She quarrelled with me over bringing Mary along, but how was I to know we'd be together all the evening. She was no less melancholy when I told her that she'd not have kept Harold for long, and neither would Mary. His sort considered themselves a cut above servant girls. 'Skivvies' were all right for an evening out and to be seduced if possible, but certainly not for a permanent relationship. I was surprised when he stuck to Mary for two months.

I had a letter from Rose asking why it was such a long time since she'd seen us. Rose seemed to forget that though she was free every day, Mary and I had only our allotted time off. I went on my own to see her as Mary said she couldn't possibly put Rose before Harold – she didn't know then that one more evening was the last she would ever have with the philandering counterhand.

Rose seemed slightly more cheerful than when I'd last seen her, and she told me she was nearly three months pregnant. Because of this, Gerald had been ever so nice and kind, making her rest and coming home early from his office I thought that Rose looked far from well, very pale and edgy. I told her that she ought to get all the fresh air she could, but Rose complained that she had nowhere to go and she'd no friends but Mary and me. She couldn't come to our places and was sick to death of walking around Hampstead on her own. She was sure that she'd have been happier as a parlourmaid and often wished she was down below stairs. I discounted that melodramatic statement. Rose would never give up the life of ease and comfort that she had now, and who would? Certainly I wouldn't have done if I'd had the same luck. Mrs Wardham had been to see her and she was ever so nice and kind. All these 'ever so's' grated on me, but it must be far worse for Gerald who heard them every day. It seemed strange to me that after months of hearing Gerald's public school accent and polished speech, her way of speaking hadn't altered in the least. Mrs Wardham had brought up some books for Rose; I was sure that she'd never even read the one I'd lent her.

The news from Redlands was that Mr Wardham was still enraged over Gerald's marrying a servant; he'd cast off his son for good and never wanted to see him again. Such was Mr Wardham's temper – never mild at the best of times but now positively evil – that Mr Burrows had given in his notice. For Madam's sake, he'd put up with harsh words and insults, but when it came to having a clothes-brush flung at him, human nature could stand no more. Rose and I giggled as we visualised the pompous and stately Burrows trying to dodge a clothes-brush. I was just saying goodbye to Rose when, much to my embarrassment, Gerald came in. Although I was no longer a servant in his mother's house and he had no jurisdiction over me, yet I was still a servant and, as such, felt distinctly inferior. Such was the vast social, educational and financial gap between above and below stairs, it was almost impossible to feel at ease unless the rigid distinctions were maintained. Rose hadn't yet managed the transposition; she was living in a kind of limbo – though I flattered myself that given her chance, I'd have made a go of it.

I could see that her husband wasn't pleased to see me as a visitor in his house, and comparing my clothes with the expensive ones Rose was wearing, I suppose I must have looked like a poor relation. Even though I was now earning £45 a year, I couldn't afford to buy expensive outfits. As I left, Rose whispered to me to come again soon and to bring Mary.

14

By the time I was in my next temporary job, the General Strike had started. One of my history books describes the strike as 'one of the most controversial and significant events of the inter-war years', but at the time it made little or no impression or difference to us in domestic service. We had so few free hours outside the basement that our need of transport was minimal and, as for the news, they had a radio above stairs and scraps of information from this were retailed to us. Not that the aged housemaid and parlourmaid would have been at all interested in the strike even if we'd had a radio below stairs. Mrs. Hunter-Jones was one of the worst kind of employers; haughty and overbearing in manner, she provided the absolute minimum for the comfort of the servants. We had no servants' hall, so in what was very limited leisure time we had to sit in the kitchen. Madam had provided just three chairs; if Mary or Gladys came to see me one of us had to stand up. Perhaps that was Madam's way of discouraging visitors. She'd also provided us with three books; the Bible, *Pilgrim's Progress* and *Little Women*. This latter, judging by the tattered cover, was the only one that previous servants had opened – though for my part I preferred John Bunyan and read him many times. When I added my own book to this extensive library – I was reading *Felix Holt the Radical* – the housemaid said Madam wouldn't like to see that book in the kitchen. Violet, who was sixty-three, had never in her life read such a book, but the word 'Radical' was enough to convince her that it wasn't a suitable book for a servant to read. Most employers provided the Bible for their servants; I suppose they were acting on the assumption that a knowledge of the hardships of life in the Old Testament, coupled with words on a paradisal after-life in the New, compensated us for our somewhat dreary existence below stairs.

We did have two pictures and a text hanging on the wall in our kitchen. One picture showed Elijah rising to heaven, and the other, Commander James Wolfe dying at the battle of Quebec. The text stated: IN ALL LABOUR THERE IS PROFIT, BUT THE TALK OF THE LIPS TENDETH ONLY TO PENURY. If that was true, there was little prospect of penury in our kitchen as Violet and Lily hardly ever spoke either to each other, or to me. Poor Lily and Violet, after twenty-five years in the same place in service, had expected to retire on an annuity; in fact, this had been promised by their employer. But, no will, no annuity. It just shows that you need to see written evidence of an assured future. Now, at sixty-three and sixty-five respectively, they had little choice of jobs; hence Mrs Hunter-Jones. I'd no intention of staying long, the place was too much like *Bleak House*.

Mary came to see me. She was thinking of leaving her job because the cook and butler were going to be married. I couldn't see what difference that need make to Mary, presumably her duties wouldn't change just because the cook and butler were entering into a legal partnership – according to Mary they'd long had an illegal one. Mary said the butler was a pompous bore and the cook, judging by the way she extracted commission from the tradesmen, must be a minor member of the Mafia. The prospect of a holy alliance between those two was more than Mary could stomach. She'd had a letter from Rose who'd just returned from a visit to her parents. Rose wrote that her father was very bitter about conditions up there. Although the General Strike had been called off, the miners were still out and Uncle Fred and his five kids were suffering. Public opinion might be sympathetic to the miners, but sympathy didn't put a wage in Uncle Fred's pocket or food in his kids' bellies. Her father said that the only man who cared about the working classes was Ernest Bevin. And when Rose got back to London, with her father's opinions and her own tales of woe, Gerald wasn't in the least understanding or kind about her anxieties. All he said was that nobody paid him for not working, and Rose's father would sing a different tune if he was one of the bosses. Also, Rose wasn't feeling well. Her pregnancy was causing her legs to swell – 'she should see my mum's after a dozen of them', said Gladys – and Gerald, who'd been ever so nice and kind when he first knew about the baby, now just snapped at her every time she complained. She was sure he didn't care for her now that she'd lost her figure.

'I don't know about you, Margaret,' said Mary, 'but I get a bit tired of listening to, or reading about her complaints. When she was the parlourmaid, Rose was such a nice girl. She was always happy and willing to help out with any extra job. However disagreeable Mr Hall was, Rose never took offence but always gave him a soft answer. But now that she's no longer one of us, she's completely changed. It's nothing now but moans and groans. And we don't really feel comfortable in her home as she hovers between being one of us and one of them. If you ask me, it's a great pity that marriage ever happened. Rose was happier in her right place. Now she doesn't seem to know where that is.'

I agreed with Mary, but at the time I couldn't worry overmuch about the problem of Rose as I'd fallen violently in love with the young man who called with the groceries. Paul was nearly six foot tall, with masses of dark wavy hair, and we used to talk and laugh in the kitchen every time he called. With two such miseries as Violet and Lily, that was about the only time there *was* laughter in the kitchen. I never thought he'd ask me to go out with him, knowing that a good-looking young man like him would have countless opportunities where girls were concerned. Although inwardly rather dismayed to discover that he was a weekend country lover, I nevertheless professed an equal enthusiasm for the delights of nature and country walks. So, every Sunday about three o'clock, we went by bus or train to somewhere on the outskirts of London and then walked for miles – or it seemed like miles to me. We ate our tea – sur l'herbe, with insects crawling below and circling above; but I was so besotted with Paul that despite the insects, I just smiled as though I was having a heavenly time. Very little about living in a city alarms me. I'm not worried about the noise, the dirt and dust, the crowded streets or the hazards in dodging the traffic. But for some reason, the countryside fills me with apprehension. Every cow looks belligerent; there may be snakes in the grass or minor tarantulas, and ditches and barbed wire seem to be everywhere. But above all it is the absolute silence that is menacing, heralding some cataclysmic upheaval in nature. The fact that this upheaval never takes place in no way lessens my apprehension. On my free weekday afternoon and evening, Paul took me to the pictures. He didn't dance, which I felt was extremely fortunate for me, as I knew that I'd suffer agonies of jealousy to see him holding another girl. This idyll lasted about a month; its end hastened, if not caused by me. In the beginning, what made Paul like me was my wit and laughter, but as soon as I fell in love these qualities were no longer in evidence. He was constantly being subjected to long searching interrogations on what he did in the evenings when he wasn't with me, and such was the intensity of the emotions I felt about him that I could no longer be light-hearted. Naturally, he got browned off sharing his country walks with a tragedy queen and, nervous of the probable scene if he cast me aside in any dramatic way, he simply stopped coming with the groceries. Shortly after that I decided to give Mrs Hunter-Jones a month's notice, for apart from the fact that the new grocery boy was only fifteen and pale and pimply, I was fed-up with the place in other ways. As companions, Violet and Lily were a dead loss; their only conversation was about their 'dear mistress' whom they'd served faithfully for twenty-five years. They were convinced that she *had* left them an annuity but the wicked nephew had destroyed the will. No amount of explaining that even if their dear mistress had kept the will in the house, a solicitor would have known the contents, altered their conviction that they'd been victims of a crime. Mrs Hunter-Jones objected to my going out for an hour in the evening, even though I'd done all my work and was only going to see a friend who was also a cook. Looking around at the 'comforts' she provided in our kitchen, Madam espied George Eliot's book and remarked that she wouldn't have thought I'd have wanted to read a book by that author. Thinking she meant the book was too erudite for me – a great many employers seemed to think that the inferiority of servants extended to their being dim-witted – I said that I'd been reading books since I was nine years old.

'Surely your mother would never have books in your home written by a woman who lived in sin?'

'I cannot see, Madam, how George Eliot's private life should make any difference. *Felix Holt* is a good story. Besides, all that happened years ago.'

'Immorality is still immorality whenever it took place, Cook. In my opinion, such a book should not be placed next to the Bible.'

Like many people, Madam paid lip-service to the Bible without literally carrying out some of its precepts, such as 'Love one another and forgive your enemies'. Violet and Lily believed implicitly in the Garden of Eden and an eventual Paradise where we would all be equal in the sight of God. To them it was almost blasphemy that I should point out the monstrous injustice of such a concept. The rich had had their paradise here below; they'd had an earthly life of ease and pleasure. Surely people like us could expect to be the privileged class up above?

I'd made up my mind to leave London for a while and go back to Brighton. Although I'd be sorry to leave Gladys and Mary, my friend Olive was in service in Hove. Besides, there was a good train service between Brighton and London, I could easily travel there and back on my half-day. Before my month's notice was up, Mary got engaged to Alf, the odd-job man where she worked.

And with what pride and joy did Mary announce the event to

me. To be actually engaged with the ring on her finger and to a man who not only had a regular job, but made a bit extra on the side. Wasn't she the lucky one! What did it matter that Alf was nearly fifteen years older than her, was only five foot three inches tall, and dropped his aitches; once they were married she'd soon alter that.

I was about to say she'd have some trouble trying to change the first two points, but thought Mary would perhaps be annoyed. I did feel envious now. First Rose getting married, now Mary engaged; I seemed to be the odd one out. We went to see Rose to tell her the good news, taking a bottle of champagne with us. With the happy event so near, Rose said she daren't drink champagne, the gassiness gave her the wind and upset the baby in the womb. When I told her that my mother had drank no end of fizzy lemonade and port when she was carrying, with no ill effects, Rose loftily answered that not all babies were alike. I suppose the heir to the Wardhams would have such a delicate system, that it wouldn't stomach lemonade and port. Rose showed us the nursery that Mrs Wardham had prepared for the baby; it was like a little palace. Pale wallpaper patterned with pink and blue rosebuds – to be ready for either sex, I suppose – a lovely wickerwork cradle and a white cot, and soft toys were every-where. Piles of beautifully embroidered baby clothes were in the cupboards, and in the hall was a maroon-coloured perambulater large enough for triplets. Mary and I dutifully admired everything and then drank all the champagne. We felt really gay and reckless, Rose had made friends with a young mother whom she'd met while walking on Hampstead Heath; she came in to see Rose while we were there. Jill Hurst had twins, a boy and a girl, now a month old. She lamented the fact that they weren't in the least alike; it was just pushing two separate babies around instead of a pair. Her Laurence was minding them at the moment and so he should, he'd helped to make them; and for all the pleasure that *she'd* got out of it, he could lay off in future unless he took precautions. Rose looked shocked at this frank statement and apparent lack of maternal love. Jill had been married for five years before the twins arrived, and she talked about married life as though it was like living in an institution with rigid rules and laws.

'I was only eighteen when I got married to Laurence and I'd known him only three months. My parents were against the idea but I made so much fuss that Daddy gave in. I had a white wedding with six bridesmaids in pale yellow, and a reception for two hundred people. We went to Italy for our honeymoon and honestly I had no knowledge of sex at all. Mummy never mentioned the subject and always looked so embarrassed when I asked her anything. Our wedding night was awful, Laurence just got on top of me without even kissing and caressing me first, and then he got angry because I didn't know what to do. I simply cried and cried. And he's always been the same; only now if I don't want him, I don't let him come near me. I tell him that if only he was as good at making love as he is at making money, he'd be something like a man.'

Well! these revelations amazed Mary and me, and Rose was beyond speaking. Nowadays, such frank disclosures of a sexually inadequate partner would occasion little or no comment but, in 1926 very few females openly discussed what went on behind the bedroom door. It was obvious that Jill came from an upper middle-class family, so I was pleased that Rose kept silent about Mary and me being domestic servants. Perhaps it would have made no difference to Jill, but to many people there was a social stigma attached to being a 'skivvy'. And there never would be any dignity to the job while it continued being caricatured in *Punch* and on the stage. Most plays of those days seemed to portray servants as figures of fun; idiotic and illiterate.

15

My reference from Mrs Hunter-Jones wasn't entirely satisfactory. Although she didn't denigrate my cooking capabilities, she mentioned that I went out at unauthorised times. Nevertheless, from my next employer I asked, and received, a wage of £52 a year, which was good money in those days, and I had a whole day off every month. As in this house servants could never be free on Fridays, Saturdays and Sundays, Mrs Bishop had to offer high wages as an inducement to get servants. Most girls wanted their alternate Sunday off, especially if they were courting; but after my unfortunate experience with Paul, I was fancy free.

Mrs Bishop had two sons but one of them was in Australia. Not that he wanted to be there, but having forged his father's name on a cheque, he had to choose between going to prison or being exiled to Australia as a 'remittance man', receiving £8 a month from his father so long as he stayed put there. Rumour had it that the butler, who left Mrs Bishop's service shortly after the son had departed, had also gone to Australia – perhaps that was the reason she now had a parlourmaid instead of a manservant.

The only man employed was the chauffeur, who used to drive Mr and Mrs Bishop to London on a Tuesday, stay up there and bring them back on Friday evening. From then on it was dinner parties every night until the next Tuesday. Mrs Bishop, Italian by birth and about sixty years old, made great endeavours, by means of excessive make-up and hair dyes, to appear about half her age. Every weekend there were pretty young men staying in the house, referred to by Mrs Bishop as 'darling Beppo, Cosimo and Tomaso', and at these weekends, they lived off the fat of the land. Occasionally Madam would ask me if I minded them coming into the kitchen to make an Italian dish, and with shrill cries and chattering nineteen to the dozen they'd flit around my kitchen wearing blue, green or red shirts, appearing, as they darted about, like brightly-plumaged birds. I liked all of them, but especially one called Nicolo who came from Siena, had laughing brown eyes and sang all the time. Whenever the others weren't around, Nicolo tried to seduce Hilda, the parlourmaid, and me. Given the chance, he'd have made love in the kitchen, larder, servants' hall, or even in a bed. But Hilda and I knew that he wasn't the marrying kind. Once Mr Bishop invited two of *his* friends, young Germans, but they didn't get on with Madam's Italians. Nicolo said what could you expect of Prussians who stuffed themselves with Frankfurter sausage, and had no idea of, or the temperament for, tenderness. Ah! Italy was the land of love, sunshine and song. Hilda remarked that if Italy was such a paradise, it was funny he was living in England; with Madam more than twice his age, surely the opportunity for romance in this house was non-existent. Nicolo just shrugged his shoulders and said, 'What would you?' Hilda and I related stories to him, mostly imaginary, of the highly desirable and romantic Englishmen that we met at dances; nice young men who would never dream of dancing attendance on an elderly woman just because she was wealthy. But Nicolo was shrewd enough to ask why, if we knew such men, we were still working as domestics. Why didn't we get married? Iris, the housemaid, was in fact engaged, to a man in the fire-brigade, a very strait-laced young man called Stanley – abbreviated to Stan by Iris. Although Stan had that most desired requisite, a regular and permanent job, neither Hilda nor I envied Iris being actually engaged – and with a ring to show. We thought her Stanley no great catch as a partner for life. He was a strict chapel-goer and, when not on Sunday duty, he ran a Bible class in the afternoon and a Young Men's Fellowship in the evening. Hilda and I agreed that viewed objectively these were admirable occupations, but we'd no wish to share in them. Iris did occasionally come dancing with us but this had to be kept a secret from Stan, who'd have strongly disapproved. She said Stan looked so lovely in his uniform and shiny brass helmet. Hilda and I had an hilarious session working out an evening of connubial bliss for Iris and Stan. After a delicious dinner cooked by Iris – though at the moment she couldn't cook a sausage – Stan would sit down in his favourite arm-chair, wearing his shiny brass helmet and holding the Bible, and read the Proverbs to Iris; then after drinking their cocoa they could retire to bed and sleep the sleep of the just. Two years later Iris did marry him and they had eight children, so obviously Stan wasn't averse to a little light entertainment.

Mary wrote to me with the news that Rose had just had a baby girl, so I took my whole day off and went to London to see her. She was in a very expensive nursing home, where visitors were allowed to call at any time, but if I'd known that Gerald's mother was going to be there, I'd have postponed my visit. However, I didn't feel too embarrassed because she was kind and pleasant, and very soon departed so that I could talk to Rose and admire the baby and the presents. Rose being so very good-looking I expected to see a pretty baby, but Victoria Helen – as she was called – had her father's features, which included a rather large nose. There were presents from Miss Helen, Sarah, Violette and Mrs Buller, but nothing whatever from Mr Wardham, who still refused to recognise Rose as a daughter-in-law.

Gerald and his partner were doing so well with their business that they'd decided to form a company and start exporting. The house in Hampstead was to be sold because Gerald wanted to buy a proper country house where he could keep a couple of horses and join a golf club. Rose should have been delighted with all this pros-perity, but it only induced a feeling of terror, and she wept as she said she'd neither wanted, nor expected, to live in that way. She'd thought that Gerald would get an ordinary job and they'd live in a cosy little house where Ma and Pa could stay with her occasionally. Now they never would, because her pa was bitter against people who were wealthy enough to employ servants; and he said that if he'd known Gerald was going to be a money-grabbing boss, he'd never have agreed to his Rose marrying him. It was useless to point out to Rose that there was no special merit attached to living in a poverty-stricken slum and denouncing the rich. She'd moved away from that life and should adapt to her surroundings. But Rose just couldn't, her heart was still in the little back-street in Manchester. And now, she moaned, if they moved from Hampstead, Mary and I would never come to see her and, while we were in service, she couldn't visit us. Leaving fervent promises that we'd still keep in touch, I went to see Mary.

But even there I found no joy, for Mary, having quarrelled with her Alf, was far from happy.

'I'm sure he's not faithful to me, Margaret. We went to the pictures on Sunday and when he kissed me goodnight I could smell perfume on his coat and there was a long golden hair on the lapel. And when I asked about it, he just laughed and said that the perfume was hair oil he'd spilled on his coat and the hair must have blown on to him. I wish he wasn't a window-cleaner then he wouldn't have the chance to meet so many women. They're always giving him cups of tea and making a fuss of him. When we get married I'll get him to change his job.'

I was about to say that in the first place it was suspicious that a thirty-five year old was unmarried, and if Mary kept nagging him he'd remain unmarried, but then I realised Mary didn't want advice, she wanted sympathy.

'They're away upstairs,' said Mary, 'and the others won't mind if I go out for a couple of hours. Let's go round to Aunt Ellie's, old Mack isn't too well and we'll cheer him up.'

I think the last thing old Mack wanted was two lively young women around. He'd married Aunt Ellie because he was lonely, but Aunt Ellie's exuberance was rapidly wearing him out, as she made him take her to theatres, cabarets and out shopping. She thought that in making Mack 'see life', it was doing him good.

'I don't want the poor old blighter to leave me a lot of money. I want him to enjoy his wealth. He worked hard enough to get it and he deserves a bit of fun.'

But Mack, now that he was old, was working much harder in spending his money, than he had worked in acquiring it. I believe he'd have been much happier sitting in an armchair by the fireside with Aunt Ellie sitting opposite. Unfortunately, Aunt Ellie wasn't a fireside person. She did care about old Mack, but loved to have a crowd of young people around. There were several sitting around drinking sherry and putting records on the gramophone and Mary rapidly cheered up after drinking two large gin-and-tonics. Discovering that I was without a young man of my own, Ellie said she had just the right person for me, a terribly sweet young man, so *very* nice, who was training to be a chef; we'd have something in common as I was a cook. Remembering Steve, the last young man she'd introduced to me, and what a wash-out he had turned out to be with his passion for dominoes, I was sceptical about her 'terribly sweet young man'. It was easy for him to be nice to attractive Ellie with an old wealthy husband; to be nice to me, just a cook below stairs, was an entirely different proposition. However, Ellie brought the charmer over to me and I was agreeably impressed with his looks. Roy Latimer seemed to like me too for he talked to me for the rest of the evening, came to Victoria Station to see me off, and asked if he could come down to Brighton to see me on the Sunday. I had to tell him that we were never free at weekends so he arranged to come down on the Wednesday evening. I was in seventh heaven that a young man should come all the way to Brighton just to see me.

16

Even Hilda, normally rather indifferent to young men, admitted that Roy Latimer was quite something. And he liked an occasional drink in a pub which was a great improvement on my previous boyfriend, George. When I went out with him we were passers-by where pubs were concerned. The only drawback was Roy working in London and me some fifty miles away, but Aunt Ellie promised to keep an eye on him and ensure his affections remained towards me.

Life was far from dull working for Mr and Mrs Bishop. He was a pleasant man though, as I have written in an earlier book, he had some peculiar tendencies. As for Madam, years of living in England had not subdued her fiery Latin temperament. Apart from her normal retinue of young men, other young lovers came and went away at fairly frequent intervals. One such was a handsome young man called Clive, who now and again got a small part in films. Madam called Nicolo and his new compatriots, her cicisbeos, but this Clive got special treatment, much to the fury of the others. We would hear them exploding in our kitchen:

'Girls, who is this Clive? (they pronounced his name, Cleeve). He is a nothing, a nobody, he is not simpatico. Our dear lady buys him clothes and shoes and he does not care for her; it is only for her money that he cares. He must not stay here.'

Considering that most weekends they got free board and lodging, we felt that they were hardly in a position to criticise another hanger-on. But Clive didn't last very long in any case; his departure was expedited by Mr Bishop who, on receiving the bills not only for Clive's finery, but for a very expensive gold watch as well, became totally incensed. His quarrel with Madam was really something and her histrionics could be heard all over the house.

I left Mrs Bishop's not only because I wanted to go back to London, but also because I now felt that I was an experienced enough cook to have a kitchenmaid to help me. I consulted the *Morning Post* and got a job in Knightsbridge where there were seven servants – nine if one included the chauffeur and an odd-job man. Madam told me the previous cook had left to get married, which was reassuring to hear. If prospective employers told you that their servants had left only to look after aged or ailing parents, then you immediately became suspicious of the job; for that was nearly always the excuse you gave to leave a situation you disliked. I'd used it myself, and later on in my married life I left so many daily jobs because my mother had broken her leg, Mum might have been a centipede.

Madam had a butler and a parlourmaid. Most high-class and wealthy families employed a butler and a parlourmaid in preference to two parlourmaids. A butler gave tone to the house. The middle-classes had parlourmaids only. Madam's butler, Mr Baines with his stately demeanour and grave mien, would have made a perfect stage butler – though the audience would probably have taken him for a caricature. But Mr Baines was never in the least pompous below stairs. He was always making us weep with laughter with his anecdotes about those above stairs – though he was never malicious. Unfortunately for the servants, Mr Baines was leaving in two months' time as his brother and sister-in-law were starting a small hotel and he was going to be the head waiter there.

'How many waiters will there be, Mr Baines?' we asked.

'Just me and a boy to start with,' he laughed. 'So, you see, I'll automatically be the head waiter.'

At the time of my arrival, Mr Baines was involved in a voluminous correspondence with the shop that had sold some woollen socks to him, and also with the company that had made the woollen socks. Mr Baines asserted they had shrunk to about half their original size, though he had washed them only in Lux. The shop and the company letters were very short and legal, but those Mr Baines had written, copies of which he showed me, covered several pages and went off into wild flights of fancy about a butler's position being in great peril if, in the course of his duties, his feet were constricted by socks which were not only matted, but too small. I reckon the firm should have sent him a few pairs gratis, if only because his letters must have made them laugh.

Mr Baines had been married to a German cook, whose parents kept a small shop in the East End of London. Although they'd been there for years, they were subjected to much abuse and harassment during the 1914–18 war, so when the war was over they went back to Westphalia and their daughter, Mr Baines' wife, went with them.

'Suppose you wanted to marry again, Mr Baines? Could you get a divorce now your wife's in Germany?'

'Oh, Cook, I'd never want to marry an English woman – no disrespect to you, of course,' he added hastily, 'My Martha could make the best pumpernickel you've ever tasted.'

'Pumpernickel! whatever's that? I've never heard of it. Something to do with pumpkins, I suppose, Mr Baines?'

'Dear, dear. Never heard of it and you a cook too. Pumpernickel is delicious rye bread. Martha occasionally used to make it especially for me. Now,' he said mournfully, 'I expect she's making it every day over there in Westphalia.'

Having a kitchen maid was a help; no more vegetables to prepare, kitchen tables and floor to scrub and washing-up to do; but it didn't take Bessie long to realise that I was not like the previous cook who shouted at, and harried her. Consequently, Bessie became slow and lazy and, rather than nag at her, I'd do the jobs myself. This wasn't good training for Bessie and could only lead to her being a slovenly cook. But I was happy enough because my romance with Roy was going well. We met on every occasion my free time coincided with his. We even got as far as talking about when he'd finished his training as a chef, then we might work in the kitchens of a smart hotel. We often went to Aunt Ellie's with Mary, whose engagement to Alf seemed likely to come to an end. Alf continually made excuses that doing two jobs made him too tired to go out in the evenings. Ellie made a fuss of Roy and me, assuring us that old Mack liked to see and hear young people, it made him feel alive. That might have been true, but it certainly didn't *keep* him alive as he died about three months after my return to London. There must have been about forty people at his funeral and Ellie spared no expense to give Mack a great 'send-off'. There were black ribbon-bedecked horses, many carriages and wreaths, and Ellie had designed a stone which later on would be placed on the grave. It was to be inscribed; DEAR MACK, HE ALWAYS DID HIS DUTY. RIP. Malicious tongues said that his duty was to depart hastily from life leaving Ellie all his money; but that was after circumstances debarred them from the use of Ellie's house and hospitality. Until he became too old to keep up with Ellie, I'm sure that Mack very much enjoyed life and never regretted marrying someone so much younger. Perhaps on his own he would have lived longer, but he might not have been so happy.

After the funeral Ellie dispensed a lavish amount of food and drink; we drank affectionately to Mack's life, death and probable destination. Apart from £250 left to a cat's home – Mack loved cats, as do I – all his money went to Ellie. She was now a fairly wealthy woman; and it was easy to see that with her lively nature and love of excitement, plus the money, her widowhood would not be of long duration.

Our new butler, a Mr Kite, was a very different person from lively Mr Baines who, in our servants' hall, ceased to be a butler and became just a very pleasant man. Mr Kite was somewhat prosy and never ceased to be a butler, albeit kindly condescending, even when he was below stairs with us six females.

Perhaps he thought that a dignified presence was the safest in purely female company – though I'm not sure that Odette, the lady's maid, was pure judging by the tales she told us about her native village in Provence. When her year with Madam was over she was going back home, and her younger sister, Yvonne, would take her place. I think Odette missed Mr Baines's frivolous conversation; she certainly scoffed at Mr Kite, saying scornfully, 'What a name, Kite. That man has never flown high in his life. Que diable! Il n'est pas pour moi. Quelle banalité.'

It was true that most of Mr Kite's contribution to our 'after dinner' conversation consisted of anecdotes about the high-class families he'd been butler to. A first hearing of these stories could be endured, but repeated telling at every opportunity was wearisome. Odette, to whom butlers were no more important than kitchen-maids – she'd not been in domestic service long enough to comprehend the rigid hierarchy below stairs – ruthlessly interrupted poor Mr Kite whenever he embarked upon a twice-told tale by saying, impatiently, 'N' importe. Nous savons tout ça'. He'd no idea what she meant but it effectively silenced him. Nevertheless, as he'd been in service from the time he left school at thirteen, Mr Kite was a very experienced butler and looked very smart in the uniform that Madam provided. None of us had to buy our uniforms, though we could choose what colours we liked. In fact, Madam provided a great many comforts for the servants; separate bedrooms, bathroom, a light and airy kitchen and a well-furnished servants' hall. We even had a bookcase in the room with proper books in it. I wasn't the only reader; for Mr Kite was pleased to find books on the shelves by Henty and W. W. Jacobs. There were also several books by Benjamin Disraeli, which at that time I found rather heavy-going to read, though I liked the many striking phrases. With my usual vanity and big-headedness, I wrote down a lot of the brilliant expressions and tried to memorise them. I had visions of uttering these bons mots when I was at a party or other social gathering, but the idea was another of my failures. In the first place, most of the people I met had never even heard of Disraeli and secondly, when I did quote him, it never seemed anything like as witty as in the book.

For all this comfort and fairly high wages, Madam expected good service from her servants – as she had a right to. She didn't take a personal interest in us, but that wasn't necessary. She looked after our physical well-being in every possible way, and I for one appreciated a kitchen stocked with everything one needed for cooking. I thought of poor old Violet and Lily toiling for Mrs Hunter-Jones and living in dreary and spartan conditions. This place was a world apart by comparison. One day Elsie, the head housemaid, asked me if I minded the previous cook, now Mrs Peek, coming to have tea with us. To my surprise, Mrs Peek had little praise for Madam. After complaining about Madam's idiosyncrasies, such as wanting dishes made differently from the way she, Mrs Peek, had been taught to make them, and the cook having to wear a clean apron every day, Mrs Peek said:

'Would you believe that in the five years I worked here, Madam had no idea that I was courting, and engaged to be married. When I gave my month's notice, Madam was very surprised. She said, "Oh, Cook, why do you want to leave?" And when I told her I was getting married, she didn't even ask what sort of job my fiancé had.'

Although I kept quiet, I saw no reason why Madam should show an interest in her servants' private affairs. I much preferred a situation where, so long as your work was satisfactory, there were no enquiries as to what you did in your free time. Madam wasn't even aware that Elsie, who was about thirty-five, had been engaged for seven years – and I'd have thought Elsie was hardly aware of it after all that time. Seven years, I just couldn't imagine it. Elsie's home was in a remote village in Kent and her fiancé worked on a farm there. She saw him only once a month when she had her whole day off and went home. As far as I could tell, both Elsie and her Jack were perfectly happy with the arrangement. By careful saving and spending, she now had a chest of linen at home and a bottom drawer filled with underwear. No frills or furbelows, just plain cotton and wincyette as befitted the farmer's wife she hoped to be eventually. There was an occasion when Elsie returned from one of her monthly visits and Odette teased her, asking did she and Jack have l'amour. Elsie replied stiffly that her Jack was a gentleman; when he stood at the altar his bride would be a virgin. Afterwards Odette said to me, 'Je pense qu'il a les pieds glacés.'

I'd picked up a bit of French from Violette but all I understood of that sentence was 'think' and 'cold', so I thought Odette was referring to the sexual part of Jack's anatomy. When I replied, 'Is it ever cold there?' I wouldn't have thought so,' it caused her much merriment.

My friend Mary had little cause for merriment as her engagement to Alf was off. She'd given in her notice because she couldn't bear now to see Alf every morning. To add to her misery and rage, Alf didn't seem to mind; he still went whistling around doing his odd jobs, just as though there had never been anything between him and Mary. We decided to visit Rose before she moved from the house in Hampstead to the palatial establishment in Surrey. As Mary said, in Hampstead we could use the front door; in the country house we'd probably end up in the stables.

17

Now that Rose had a baby she seemed more contented, though still averse to the idea of moving into a large country house. She wanted to stay with her parents in Manchester while all the moving went on. But Gerald was against the idea, saying that a back-street in the slums of Manchester was not good for Victoria Helen; and furthermore, he wasn't having his child acquiring a Mancunian accent. Considering the child was only a few months old, I couldn't see how she could possibly be affected by accent.

One couldn't in truth describe Victoria Helen as a pretty baby for, as I've said, she had the Wardham features, and to a marked degree. It was to be hoped that in disposition she wouldn't take after her grandfather. It very much grieved Mrs Wardham that she couldn't have Rose and the baby to stay at Redlands, but the awful Mr Wardham would never allow it. Neither Mary nor I could visualise Rose as one above stairs in the very house where she'd been a servant, and certainly those below stairs would object to waiting on her. They might not begrudge Rose her new-found affluence, but they wouldn't want her under their noses, so to speak.

Over tea, Rose told us that there was to be a house parlourmaid and a cook general at the country house, as well as a woman from the village who was coming three times a week to do the rough.

Gerald was thinking of going into politics. Ever since the huge demonstration in Hyde Park against the unfair – or believed by the public to be unfair – treatment of Sacco and Vanzetti, Gerald had been talking about the dangers of Communism getting a hold in England. As Rose hadn't known that Sacco and Vanzetti were Italian communists on trial in America – or even that two such men were in the news, as she seldom looked at a newspaper – she was only bored by her husband's convictions. As far as I could see, marriage to one of the upper class had not improved Rose in any way. Her outlook on life was still as narrow, her social and intellectual understanding almost non-existent, and spiritually she was still in the slums of Manchester. But she'd changed as a friend. Although she still wanted to see Mary and me, she wasn't really interested in our personal life; our work, our boyfriends and life below stairs no longer concerned Rose. She really only needed us as an audience, to hear about the strains of coping with a large house and entertaining guests; and to sympathise with her about Gerald's complaints of her failings.

Mary, more prone to blunt remarks than I was, said to Rose; 'How is it that Gerald had got so rich? He didn't do well in Rhodesia, and showed no signs of making money when we were at Redlands, yet now he seems to be rolling in the stuff. I wouldn't have thought he had it in him.'

Rose took no offence at hearing this, and in fact agreed; but in her opinion it was Gerald's partner that was the real brains.

'From the time he met Ronald Frost, Gerald's luck has changed. Now everything they do seems to make money. From having one little office in the City, they now have a whole floor. I don't much care for Ron, he's always making jokes that I can't understand, but Sheila's ever so nice. She's got ever so many friends and sometimes they all come here for tea. Now I'm going to have a proper staff, I'll be able to have people to dinner without having to worry about the work.'

On the way back Mary, who I could sense had become irritated listening to Rose's conversation, said, 'Margaret, we'll not go there any more. Notice how Rose never has any of her posh friends call while we're in the house.' And mimicking Rose's voice, Mary added, 'I'll have people to dinner. We don't have supper, nothing so common now I have a staff.' Then, abruptly changing the subject, Mary asked me if I'd seen Roy lately.

'Sure I see him whenever he and I are free at the same time. Why do you ask?'

'He seems to spend a lot of time at Aunt Ellie's. The last three times I've been there, your Roy and Aunt Ellie seemed to be very friendly. I'd just thought I'd warn you, Margaret.'

'Warn me of what? You know your aunt has always liked young people around. You can't possibly be suggesting that there's something going on between Roy and your aunt. Why, she's older than him.'

'Not all that much older. And don't forget Aunt Ellie's got money now.'

I parted from Mary feeling extremely upset and, although I said to myself that Mary was just being catty because she'd lost Alf, in my heart I knew it wasn't so, Mary wasn't like that. I went over all the details of the previous weeks. Had Roy seemed any different? No, of course he hadn't; Mary must have got the wrong impression. Of course Roy liked Ellie, but so did a lot of the young people she welcomed in her home. Roy still discussed what we would do when he'd finished his training, he was still as loving and tender when we were together. But however I tried to reassure myself that all was well, uneasiness remained. Especially so when I recollected that on two or three occasions Roy had left a note to say he'd got to work an extra shift so wouldn't be able to keep our date. Had he been telling the truth?

In a way it was fortunate that Madam was doing a lot of entertaining, for it kept me too busy to worry overmuch. There was to be a dinner party for eighteen people and Madam and I were planning the menu; Mr Kite was polishing the silver – or, rather, he was doing the more delicate pieces while Norma did the cutlery. He carefully inspected each fork to make sure that Norma had brushed out all the Goddard's powder. Mr Kite's importance as a butler had slightly diminished by having a parlourmaid under him; in his previous place he'd had a footman. There is more prestige attached to being a butler with a footman than a butler with a parlourmaid, however efficient she is.

Mr Kite had left his previous situation because of the goings-on between the new handsome young footman and the master above stairs. In all the years in which our butler had given honourable service to high-class families, he'd never known such a thing to happen. I think what shocked Mr Kite more than the immorality of it, was the fact that accepted traditions had been overturned, the master and servant relationship violated. Poor Mr Kite couldn't possibly continue to work in such a situation. He said to me, pompously:

'Cook, if I could bring myself to talk about what went on there, you'd never believe me. But I couldn't lower myself to utter the words.'

'Don't even try, Mr Kite,' I answered hastily, having no wish to hear a sordid saga from prosy Mr Kite. I felt sure that if the master had even smiled at his footman, Mr Kite would have interpreted it as an immoral advance.

Such inhibitions on frank speech meant nothing to Odette, who frequently entertained us with colourful – and probably embellished – tales about Provencal life. Mr Baines had always laughed whenever Odette, lacking knowledge of the English word for something she wanted to say, lapsed into French. She did this one evening while she was talking about Paris to Norma, Bessie and me. Trying to describe the street lavatories for men, she called them 'pissoirs', and Mr Kite looked really pained. He'd have us know that he'd been to France with one of his employers and had not liked the country, the people, or their customs. As for the sanitary arrangements, even in Paris they were disgusting; fancy both sexes having to use the same entrance to a lavatory – and sometimes even share it. Odette derided such opinions; 'You English are just prudes', she said. But I must admit that we too found the idea somewhat revolting.

Mr Kite often complained to me that service was no longer the same as when he was a lad. The nobility and the gentry were fading away and a high-class butler, such as he was, had sometimes to have a dozen interviews before he found the right place.

'You know, Cook, it never does to take an inferior place where you cannot take a pride in your work. Being a top-class butler means that one starts in service from the bottom and gradually works one's way up the ladder. One is not going to throw all that experience away on employers who don't appreciate a real butler. Would you believe it, Cook, in one of the situations I went after, although they advertised for an experienced butler, at the interview I discovered that not only did I have to do the work single-handed, I was expected to be handyman too. I very soon told them that I hadn't spent nearly forty years in good service to become a handyman. Ah no, Cook, it's so easy for us servants to fall into bad service; we have to be constantly on our guard. One bad employer from whom one requires a reference and the damage is done. The next employer will think the man couldn't have been much of a butler to work in such a place.'

Mr Kite's conversation was never wildly exciting and as a rule I only half listened to what he had to say. Nevertheless, I suppose he was right in what he told me; the difference between us being that if I got a bad place I didn't worry but changed it as soon as possible. But then I didn't intend to spend all my life in domestic service as Mr Kite plainly did.

The night of the dinner party was extremely hectic and for once I really hectored Bessie and made her give me more help, for I'd never before cooked for such a large party. It wasn't so much the actual cooking as getting the amounts right that worried me; a lot of food was needed to feed eighteen people. The menu was to be artichoke soup, with cream added just before serving; followed by sole normande, made with white wine and decorated with truffles. The entrée was veal cutlets and espagnole sauce, and the main course, the remove, saddle of lamb with mint sauce and redcurrant jelly – the latter bought ready-made. The sweet was cold honeycomb mould; and finally there were devilled prunes for the savoury. It all went extremely well, nothing was under-done, over-done or burnt, much to my relief. During the rush Mr Kite whispered to me that a Mrs Denver, a well-known diner-out, had particularly praised the sole normande. When it was all over, I was just thankfully sitting down for a few minutes before helping Bessie with the mounds of washing-up and getting our own supper, when who should come into the kitchen but Madam with a guest. I felt so embarrassed; all the cooking had left me as red as a peony, and the kitchen was still strewn with utensils.

Madam smiled at me, saying, 'Excuse us invading your kitchen, Cook, and don't get up; you must be feeling tired. The dinner was splendid and Mrs Denver would very much like the recipe for the sole normande.'

Mrs Denver added her thanks and they went back upstairs.

Just before she left, Mrs Denver surreptitiously slipped an envelope into the butler's hand; it was addressed to me. Inside was £5, and a message to the effect that if I ever contemplated leaving Madam, would I let her know. Mr Kite was pained at such perfidy. To be Madam's guest, eat at her table and then try to lure away one of her servants was base conduct. Besides, he knew that Mrs Denver lived in a tiny apartment with two maids, so it could hardly be for herself that she wanted a cook.

'In that case, Mr Kite,' I told him, 'Mrs Denver's a procuress. But instead of procuring for bawdy houses, she procures reliable cooks for her friends – probably for a small consideration.'

Mr Kite had received about six pounds in tips so we pooled all the money. Although the housemaids were not directly involved in the dinner party – nobody was staying the night – nevertheless Ada had helped with washing the silver in the butler's pantry, Elsie had to be on duty upstairs to tidy Madam's bedroom after the lady guests had used it, and we couldn't leave out Odette.

It was past eleven o'clock by the time we had our supper; but although we were tired, everybody was cheerful because the evening had gone well. Mr Kite even laughed at one of Odette's somewhat ribald remarks and then he told us an amusing story about when he was a second footman!

'One evening, at a very important dinner, and just as I was handing round the dish of peas to a guest, I sneezed violently, my hands shook and several of the peas shot off in all directions. There was a dreadful silence; it was too terrible, I wished that I was dead. Fred, the first footman, could hardly restrain his mirth, and the expression on the face of the old family butler gives me a nightmare still when I think of it. It wasn't my fault I sneezed, I just couldn't suppress it, but I'm certain that the martinet of a butler considered I should have choked rather than have disgraced his training.'

Coming from Mr Kite, this was quite a story and he was obviously gratified to hear us all laugh. It was the last time for quite a while that I did laugh, because the morning brought me two letters; one from Rose and the other from Roy.

18

The next morning, feeling proud and pleased by the ultimate success of the previous evening, I received a letter from Roy; and certainly I was not prepared for the shattering news it contained. How could I be, when Roy had been as kind and affectionate as usual when we'd last met. I'd forgotten Mary's warning. In the first part of his letter there was no finesse, no softening of the blow. He simply stated that he and Ellie were getting married. That they loved each other and the disparity in age made no difference to their love. I had to read it three times before I really grasped the fact that I had lost Roy. The rest of the letter was merely padding. He still liked me and hoped that I'd find a man better than he, Roy, could ever be. But we weren't really suited to each other, because as Ellie had pointed out, we were both Scorpios with possessive natures. So, if we married, neither of us would be happy. I was too upset to take much notice of this last statement; but some weeks later, gradually recovering from my broken romance and reading yet again his rejection of me, I was furious at Ellie's assumption that Roy and I were unsuited to each other. Both Scorpios indeed! I bet she couldn't even say the names of the constellations, or tell the difference between astrology and astronomy.

On the morning that I received the letter, I felt nothing but pain and grief, yet I had to hide my feelings from the servants and especially from Madam. Although she looked after our physical well-being, I could sense that she would only be irritated if she found herself involved in our personal lives.

My other letter was from Rose with the news that her Uncle Fred, the miner, despairing of finding work, was coming to London with his wife and the three youngest children. Her parents had written to say that Rose must go to see Uncle Fred and help him if possible. Rose wanted Mary and me to join her. That was so like Rose. Confronted with a situation which might prove embarrassing, her instinctive reaction was to protect herself by having friends around. Neither Mary nor I had met Uncle Fred and I felt he would hardly welcome the invasion of two strangers. Uncle Fred had said that life for the poor in London must be better than the slums of Manchester, and he liked what he'd read about the irrepressible cockney humour prevailing over the worst of circumstances.

As I said to Mary when we met, Uncle Fred would be disappointed. Like a lot of people viewing London from a distance, the city might seem a Utopia, a haven and refuge. But there *are* no Utopias, except perhaps in heaven; and by the late twenties, belief in heaven was rapidly fading – especially among the young. Agnosticism was now the thing, a non-religion. The slums of London were no more salubrious than the slums of Manchester, and as for humour: yes, given just enough to eat and a roof over their heads, perhaps cockney humour *was* irrepressible. But given an unemployed husband, one stinking room and starving children crying for food, Londoners were as miserable as any in a similar situation. Just as in the Second World War, when the newspapers printed that no amount of bombing could stop Londoners' earthy humour, that simply wasn't true. No-one, unless they were totally without emotions, could see and hear the carnage night after night and then emerge from the shelters uttering a merry quip or bawdy obscenity.

Mary, having so recently had her own romance and even engagement come to nothing, was just the friend I needed for my lamentations about my lost Roy and her Aunt Ellie. I'd given her all my advice and sympathy, now she did the same for me. Naturally, her Aunt Ellie, from now on, was an anathema to me, but Mary too declared that she would never again see the cunning, underhand woman.

'To think,' Mary declared, 'that she was always asking us to her home, trying to pair us off with young men and making out that old Mack liked company, and all the time she was picking out the next husband. I think it's awful, and poor Mack hardly cold yet.'

Mary was always prone to exaggeration, and I pointed out to her that it was to be hoped that poor Mack was cold when they put him in his coffin, never mind his grave.

'Come on, Margaret, let's find a pub where they don't take any notice of two young females on their own. We'll have a few drinks and cheer ourselves up. We'll sit and talk about men and run them all down.'

'And tell sad stories of the death of kings, how some have been deposed, some murdered by their wives,' I added; but Mary knew no Shakespeare.

She did though, say prosaically, 'We didn't get the chance to depose our boyfriends though we'd cheerfully have murdered them.'

In those days a woman seldom went into a pub, unless with her husband or boyfriend, but after looking into one or two we eventually found a large pub so crowded that we'd hardly be noticed. In fact, there were two or three females dotted around the bar, but I don't think they were there to drown their own sorrows; more to comfort any lone male whose wife didn't understand him.

Mary and I ordered two glasses of port as being a more appropriate drink than gin for two unaccompanied females. By our third glass of Sandeman's, we both began to feel that perhaps we might survive the blow that fate had dealt us; though of course life would never again be as carefree.

'You know, Margaret,' said Mary, very solemnly, 'the more I think about it, the more I feel certain there was something wrong with that Alf. Why wasn't he married? At his age most men have got a family. And why did he need two jobs? I wouldn't mind betting that he'd got a wife and kids somewhere. I reckon I've had a lucky escape – in more ways than one.' Then she added, giggling madly, 'You should have seen the way that Alf used to puff and pant when he brought in the coal-scuttles. He'd be red in the face. I reckon he'd no stamina. Just imagine him as a husband; by the time he'd climbed the stairs to the bedroom, he'd have been whacked out.'

'Well, you could have lived in a bungalow,' I said, and Mary nearly upset her port with laughing.

'As for that Roy of yours, Margaret, he wouldn't have been your type. What would you have found to talk about? The only books he ever read were Sexton Blakes. Not only that, when Aunt Ellie gave us a meal, your Roy ate his peas off a knife. Just think of a life-time sitting opposite a man who ate peas off a knife.'

I'm afraid that I wasn't consoled by those strictures on the bad habits of my lost love. If we had married, I wouldn't have been concerned with his mental prowess and, as for his eating habits, I reckoned I could have soon altered them.

Mary went babbling on about Roy being no good and he could only be marrying Ellie, a woman so much older than him, for her money. Probably he was, but one couldn't deny that Ellie was also an attractive woman. She knew how to talk to men and make them feel important.

'By the time Roy is forty,' said Mary, 'Aunt Ellie will be past it. What will he do then, I ask you?'

I neither knew nor cared about what Roy would do at forty. It was what he'd done now that concerned me. I knew that if by some miracle he was to walk through those pub doors and tell me it was all a mistake, that it was me he loved, I'd be full of joy and happiness.

Mary's laughter had attracted the attention of a young man at the next table and they were very soon talking animatedly. If I hadn't been there, I believe Mary would have got friendly with him; in spite of the fact that we were supposed to be consoling ourselves for our broken romances and therefore right off all men for ever.

Mary, who'd taken a new situation to get away from Alf, wasn't very happy in it. She'd taken a place as head housemaid in a large house in Belgravia, and found that she was expected to be a lady's maid on top of her other duties. Not that Mary would have minded, but the Madam was a harsh and overbearing woman. 'She's nothing but a parvenu', Mary had said. She didn't really know what 'parvenu' meant but had heard Mr Wardham use the expression in a contemptuous way when talking about some newcomers. Mary's employer had been left a fortune by her grandfather who'd made his money in trade; so they were neither nobility nor gentry. I suppose that Madam, having fairly recently removed herself from the mire and muck, wasn't going to fraternise with those still in it.

'She hasn't a clue how to treat servants,' Mary complained, 'Would you believe it, last week she bought two yapping Pomeranians, and in the evening rang the drawing-room bell for our butler – such a nice man – to take them out for an airing and to do the necessary. Mr Yates said, very politely, that it was no part of his duties to walk two lap-dogs round Belgravia. Then Madam had the cheek to say her dogs had a better pedigree than he, the butler, had, and he'd better look for another post. I think I'll give in my notice too, Margaret, if Mr Yates is going. Our cook is an old harridan, she treats the poor kitchenmaid like dirt. As for our servants' hall, well, I'd never ask anyone to tea there it's so awful. One small window, so it's always dark, old brown lino on the floor, dirty misshapen wicker chairs and bilious yellow-painted walls. And our bedrooms are not much better.'

I thought with complacency of our bright and comfortably furnished servants' hall and our pleasant bedrooms, each with an armchair so that we could have privacy and comfort. Even Mr Kite, who'd worked in huge establishments, admitted that more was done for the servants' comfort than any other place he'd been in. But then, being Mr Kite, he had to launch into a long and wearisome discourse as to why this should be so. For Mr Kite, like most of us, liked to think that he had left his mark wherever he had been. He didn't want me to think that he'd been of so little importance to his past employers that nothing had been done for his comfort.

'You see, Cook, when I started in domestic service, servants were ten-a-penny, you had to be good to keep your job, otherwise you get the sack because they could always get another to take your place. Nowadays, it's not so easy to get, and keep, good experienced maids and manservants. Since the war, the working class have got the idea that they're lowering themselves by working in private service. Some of this new lot wouldn't have lasted five minutes in the old days. Just imagine, Cook, in my last place we had a new housemaid; just left school she had, and when Madam spoke to her on the first morning, saying, in as nice a voice as I'm talking to you now, "Are you getting on all right, Taylor, I know this is your first place," that girl had the cheek to answer, "Yes, thank you, Mrs Mannering." I tell you, Cook, I couldn't believe my ears. I came out of the dining-room, where I was about to serve breakfast, and after Madam had gone in I told that girl off in no uncertain terms. And what, Cook, do you think that impertinent girl said? She said, "Why should I be called Taylor? I'm either Joan or *Miss* Taylor". Did you ever hear the like? And Madam such a real lady.'

Once again I resolved never to mention domestic service to Mr Kite, he was such an encyclopaedia of every aspect of it. But as his whole life had been spent in service, he had no other conversation. Still, at least he spoke good English, which was more than could be said of Rose's Uncle Fred's wife when we called on her.

19

Calling on Uncle Fred was not an experience that Mary and I would have wanted to repeat and, looking back on it, I find it hard to understand why we didn't simply refuse to go with Rose. Perhaps we were curious to see how Rose looked now, and curious to see a real coalminer – even one far removed from his natural habitat.

We met Rose at Waterloo Station. When we saw how she was dressed, we immediately protested that she was far too 'got-up' to call on an out-of-work family. Rose explained, plaintively, that her outfit was the oldest and plainest she possessed; and in any case, Uncle Fred knew that Gerald was wealthy so he wouldn't expect to see his niece looking shabby.

Her uncle and aunt, with the three children, were living in Harlesden. They had two rooms and a kitchen; the lavatory they shared with two other families. I thought the place somewhat grim; not knowing at the time that eventually I would be living in just such a place with my husband and three children – and be perfectly happy in it.

We found Rose's uncle filling in a football coupon, and he showed no signs of pleasure at being interrupted. With a first prize of £50 it was naturally important to devote time and study to the occupation. Besides, while not averse to seeing his niece, I don't suppose he'd expected a deputation. He was a short, pale, thin and wizened man, looking far older than his forty-five years. Unlike Rose's father, who hectored and harangued, Uncle Fred's thin lips were tightly closed as though he feared to speak, and he seemed to smoulder with an inward bitterness. After filling in his coupon, he put on his cap and went out; and he did not return while we were there. Mary and I were rather peeved; as we'd given up some of our sparse leisure time, we felt he ought to show some appreciation. But I suppose, he had no wish to talk to young and ignorant girls who had no real knowledge or experience of the hardships he and his family had endured.

Mary and I had brought sweets and a toy each for the children, and Rose provided what was urgently needed, money. Her aunt, Mrs Green, was a shapeless lachrymose woman who, as soon as her husband had gone, complained to us about the lack of privacy they had there.

'Back home, folks never came in your door without so much as a "by your leave". Neighbours respected each other. Even if it was only a miner's cottage, it was his castle. Once he'd shut his door, that was it. In this house, people are all the time running up and down the stairs and other people's kids open your door. I wish we were back home, I do. Father's got no sign of a job; we'd as well starve up there as down here. But Father would come.'

'Father' was, of course, her husband. Mrs Green seemed to me to be totally subservient to him. If she had any opinions, which I doubted, she never voiced them – very different from my mother, who not only had opinions but made sure that we were all aware of them.

'Hasn't Uncle Fred been offered any kind of a job yet?' asked Rose.

'Yes, he's been after two. The first was as a storesman and, although the wages were only fifty shillings a week, Father said there were about a hundred men queueing-up for the job. He didn't stand a chance. The other job he'd to know a bit of book-keeping; Father can't do with figures.'

As we departed, Rose tried to leave some money without saying anything, but Mrs Green would have none of that. Clutching the notes, she tearfully thanked Rose, saying that only because of the children would she take the money; how very hard it was to be brought so low, and Fred was so bitter about accepting charity. He'd gone into the mines when he was twelve years old and, from the time Fred's father broke his leg in the very same mine that Fred was in, Fred had practically kept his young brother and sister. And now look at him, forty-five years old, wants to work and has to swallow charity. As we walked away, our feelings of depression were not lessened by Alice, a pretty little girl about six years old, running after us to say thank you for the sweets and the present. Rose openly wept, but then she knew how hard life had been for such men as Uncle Fred; Mary and I had never even seen a coalmine. Also, I expect Rose felt the difference between her life of ease and comfort and the misery of her aunt.

But with the natural resilience of youth and, I'm afraid, the callousness of it too, we quickly became cheerful in a teashop as we consumed doughnuts and cream cakes. Mary and I wanted to know every detail about the new house. What were the servants like? How was the baby and Mrs Wardham? To give Rose her due, she did ask us what had *we* been doing before she launched into a long, and at times, incoherent account of her life. She didn't much care for the new house, it was too far from London. She was lonely, apart from the vicar and his wife, nobody called. The only people she saw were the servants, and Gerald had insisted that she was not to get on familiar terms with them. Unless they realised their employer was above them, no servant would do his work properly. Why couldn't Rose be like his mother, who not only treated servants well but had total respect for them too.

As Rose paused for breath, I thought what a dolt Gerald was. Why should he expect a girl like Rose to manage a house in the same way as his mother did. Mrs Wardham belonged to a family that for generations had employed servants; it was easy for her to know how to treat them.

Mrs Wardham engaged the servants as Rose said she couldn't for the life of her go into a registry office as an employer. This had infuriated Gerald who felt strongly that as he'd removed Rose from her servant status, she should no longer feel like one.

'I quite like Mrs Rush, the cook,' said Rose, 'she's such a help with the menus and doesn't mind if I've no idea what to order. But Flora, our house parlourmaid, she makes me feel inferior somehow. She's always saying Madam this, and Madam that. I'm really fond of young Tilly who comes in from the village to help out when there's a party; though Gerald's just like his awful father, saying that he doesn't care to have village girls in his house, they gossip afterwards'.

Rose told us that Gerald insisted on inviting his friends to the house. Some of them were business acquaintances and, as she, Rose, took no interest in his business, she'd no idea what to say to them. As for the wives, she couldn't stand them. They were painted and peroxided, called each other 'dear', and 'darling', and talked about the plays they'd seen and sweet Cecil's paintings and charming Ronnie's yacht. It was all rubbish in Rose's view. When the house was empty, she saw little of Gerald. At weekends he was out on his horse. He'd tried to get Rose to take up riding but she was terrified of sitting on a horse. This had enraged Gerald so much – especially as he'd already bought the animal – that he'd been rude enough to say that Rose's milieu was still the servants' hall; and if he, Gerald, had known what he knew now, she'd never have left it.

'He was ever so awful,' said Rose, indignantly, 'and just because I couldn't get on a horse' – for other inadequacies too, I reckoned. 'Anyway,' went on Rose, 'some of the men think Gerald's lucky to have a wife as pretty as I am. They don't expect me to know about stocks and shares; they say a pretty little head like mine shouldn't worry about money, leave money to the men. Servants' hall,' said Rose, almost venomously, one could tell the expression had rankled, 'I've long ago forgotten I was ever in one.'

She seemd oblivious of the fact that Mary and I were still in one and had no immediate prospects of removing ourselves to a higher region – or any other region at all. But then, as Mary and I philo-sophically agreed, we didn't have the 'face that launched a thousand ships', though, thank heaven, ours weren't bad enough to sink them.

Later on, when I was talking about the hardships and risks of being a coalminer, the head housemaid argued that a farm labour-er's work was just as hard and hazardous. Her Jack worked from early dawn until after sunset with no security in his job; he could be given a week's notice at any time. As for the wages, a farm labourer was the most poorly-paid of any worker.

Mr Kite interposed with one of his usual ponderous orations, 'Yes, Elsie, but you have to remember that a farm labourer's job is a healthy one; he doesn't spend hours in a dark basement at the beck and call of not just one employer, but of anybody above stairs who requires him. Your Jack may address his employers as Mr and Mrs, but I have to say Sir and Madam to everybody above stairs, even though they may be just guests; and however obnoxious the children are, they are Miss and Master. Besides Elsie, when you get married, you'll have a cheaply rented cottage and Jack can grow vegetables.'

Elsie listened to all this with growing irritation. 'One can't live on cheap rent and vegetables,' she replied, angrily. 'And with the hours of work that Jack puts in, he'll have precious little time for his own amusements.'

Odette, whose understanding of English was not yet good enough to keep pace with all the conversation, and who seemed to be obsessed by 'l'amour' – or the absence of it – did grasp the last few words, 'little time for his own amusements'. She loudly exclaimed, 'Mais non! Vous ne comprenez pas. N'importe quoi.' And then, see-ing our blank looks, Odette tried to explain in English; 'It is l'amour, the marriage, one must have time for the love.'

To Odette, amusements were synonymous with love or, if she was to be believed, they were so in her native Provençal village. She was rather scornful about Englishmen as lovers, saying they were cold, and they had no idea how to make love in the way that

Frenchmen did. Perhaps she was right, but I'm sure that Englishmen know the basics; the rest, after all, is only variations on a theme.

Afterwards, Odette – who called me Margaret, not Cook – said to me, 'Margaret, haven't you learnt any French from that book I lent to you?'

'Certainly, Odette, I now know two sentences: "En ce moment je fais des chaussettes", and "Elle éclate de rire".'

Odette certainly did the latter, as indeed did I. But of all the French phrases I could have learnt, why did I memorise, 'Just now I am knitting socks?' An absolutely useless sentence! In a wild flight of fancy, I imagine myself at some important and glittering function in Paris. Sitting next to me is a young and handsome Frenchman. Leaning towards me, gazing into my green eyes, he murmurs tenderly – in French of course – 'Ma chère, je te veux heureuse.'

And I blush and whisper, 'Merci, monsieur. Mais en ce moment je fais des chaussettes.'

Odette wasn't feeling very happy at this time because Madam was going to Holland for three weeks and taking Odette with her. They were going to Schiedam, where Mrs Van Lievden, our employer's mother, lived. Odette wasn't keen on the Dutch people, she said they had no joie de vivre. Years later, when I went to Holland, I found the Dutch people extremely friendly and helpful – and very many of them spoke good English too, which was more than could be said for the French. I strongly suspect that even when French people can understand English, they pretend to be ignorant. In their opinion, we should learn the language before venturing into their country.

While Madam was away, we servants had to get on with a massive spring-cleaning. The housemaids had to take up the carpets and beat them, brush the heavy velour curtains, wash every china ornament and polish every piece of mahogany and oak. Mr Kite and Norma had to do the dining-room carpet and all the silver, used and unused, while Bessie and I had the kitchen and scullery, servants' hall and long corridor to clean. I still had to cook for all of us, but the meals were somewhat plain while the spring-cleaning lasted.

The chauffeur, Ewan Davies, was given a holiday; as was Tom, our odd job man; though as Tom did several odd jobs in the neighbourhood, he still called in for a breakfast every morning. Ewan Davies came from Swansea and had only been in London for two years. He'd worked all his life with horses, then his boss changed to motorised transport and went bankrupt just as Mr Davies had learnt to drive. Not able to get a job in Swansea, he, like hundreds of other workless, came to London. He and his wife lived in a mews flat over the garage where the cars were kept. Although he had to wear a uniform, he did not regard himself as a domestic servant and one day, when our butler included Mr Davies in a talk about 'us domestics', Mr Davies broke in quite angrily to say that *he* wasn't a domestic servant, he didn't 'live in'. Mrs Davies was a very tiny, if extremely voluble little woman, and a splendid cook. She used to make a lovely hotpot using slices of thick smoked bacon, and her Welsh gingerbreads were just as I liked them, moist and sticky. Ewan Davies was an ardent patriot who thought that Wales was superior to the rest of the British Isles – even though he couldn't find work in his county of Glamorgan. Owen Glendower was an heroic man according to Mr Davies, but as I'd never heard of him the name meant nothing to me.

Mr Van Leivden had two cars, a Rolls Royce and an Austin. Mr Davies wasn't allowed to use the Rolls Royce for his own pleasure but, as he'd been given permission to use the Austin while they were away, he offered to take me out for a drive. Madam had told us that so long as all the work was done and either I, Elsie or Mr Kite was in the house, we could take extra time off. I thought it would be interesting to see where Rose lived, a few miles from Basingstoke, so when Mary had her free afternoon and evening, Mr Davies drove down there and arranged to collect us some hours later on his way back from visiting his wife's parents.

Mary and I never forgot that day – and emphatically not because it was enjoyable. It certainly taught me never to arrive as an unexpected visitor.

20

We left London about 2 o'clock and I think the journey took about two hours. I know that Mr Davies, a very competent driver in London, completely lost his way once we got into the country; he complained that the sign-posting was inadequate. When eventually we found the village and enquired the way to Greenlands – the name of the house – we still had half a mile to go. The house was not as large as we had visualised from Rose's description; nevertheless, it was a handsome building with weathered stone and mullioned windows, giving the impression that it had stood there for years past and would continue to do so for years ahead.

There were several cars in the drive, and as we climbed the wide steps to the front door Mary remarked, uneasily, that perhaps we should have let Rose know we were coming. I was beginning to feel the same way, even though I answered that Rose would be delighted to see us. The door was opened by the house parlourmaid, and coming from the back of the house, we could hear talking and laughter. Mary and I looked at each other and, if the maid hadn't been there, I'm sure we'd have beaten a precipitous retreat. As it was, we said that we were friends of Mrs Wardham and, as we happened to be in the neighbourhood, we would very much like to see her. The maid gave an audible sniff – 'snob,' muttered Mary – and said that Madam was entertaining guests. She left us sitting in the hall while she took in our names to Madam. The hall was very imposing; oak-panelled, with a double staircase leading up to a wide balcony; parquet-flooring and two or three Persian rugs. Looking at all this evidence of wealth and good taste – Gerald's, of course – we could see how painfully aware Rose had been made of the difference between her conditions and Uncle Fred's. Rose came running out to us and immediately Mary and I felt that here was a stranger. She really looked beautiful in a floating black chiffon dress, a three-row gleaming pearl necklace and her lovely golden hair like a halo round her face. But fortunately for us, the moment she spoke it was the same old Rose with the same old excruciating accent. She hastily removed us from the hall – and from the festivities too, as I saw that the dining-room table had been laid for eight people. We went up to her bedroom, which was decorated in pale green – Rose's favourite colour. I noticed that her taste in reading had still not progressed beyond the paperback romances, for on the bedside table was a pile of them, the top one entitled *Love's Sacrifice*.

Flora, the house parlourmaid, came in with a tea-tray looking, if that were possible, even more disapproving than when she'd ushered us into the hall. And when Rose, told her to bring some cake, as she'd discovered there was only biscuits on the tray, her sour face could have curdled the milk.

'Oh dear!' Rose lamented. 'If only you'd let me know. I never thought you'd ever come all this way to see me. Just the day when a lot of Gerald's friends are here. He and his partner have just made a lot of money – I don't know how – and Gerald's bought a new car and they're all here to look at it. Some of them are staying on to dinner too.'

'Yes, we saw the evidence as we were whisked by the door,' Mary replied, drily. 'This is the first time I've been entertained in a bedroom. And why only one bed here? Don't you and Gerald sleep together now? And where's Victoria Helen? Downstairs with the party?'

'Of course she isn't, Mary. She's staying with Gerald's mother and his aunt down in Cornwall. My mother-in-law dotes on Victoria but Gerald's father won't let her stay at Redlands. What a horrible man he is. And I have a separate bedroom because Gerald comes home late and I hate being disturbed. Besides,' and Rose blushed, 'I don't like that side of married life, being mauled about. When we were first married, I'd put my arms around him and kiss him to show my affection. But no sooner did I do that than he'd want to get on top of me. Ugh! It makes me shiver to think of it.'

'But you liked it in the beginning, Rose,' I said, 'I remember you telling us how loving Gerald was.'

'Perhaps I did, but I didn't know then that he'd want to make love so often. Why, you'd never believe, but in the first months of our marriage he'd come home at midday and expect me to go to bed with him. At midday, in the daylight. If my ma knew she'd think it disgusting. And so it is too.'

Mary and I looked at each other; and I for one remembered what young Fred had said in our servants' hall at Redlands, apropos of Rose and Gerald. 'I think that it's Gerald who will regret it'. What was Rose giving him in return for a lovely home, beautiful clothes and a life of ease? She refused to acquire an education, to read about current events; as an intellectual companion she was hopeless; now we heard that she was loth to be a bed-mate. And although she was even prettier now than when he'd fallen in love with her, Gerald had a right to expect more out of marriage than just gazing at a pretty face.

Rose went on complaining. 'Gerald wants me to have another baby, but I can't do with kids, I'm not the maternal type. He'd like to have a son; but I'm as likely to have another girl. Besides, what's the use of having a family when that father of his won't even look at them.'

Flora knocked on the bedroom door to say that Mr Wardham wished to speak to his wife. Rose went outside to speak to him and we were extremely embarrassed to hear the sound of an altercation between Rose and Gerald. I had an overwhelming desire to be somewhere else. Rose came in, looking hot and flustered, to say that she was so very sorry, she simply loved seeing us and if only we'd let her know we were coming she'd have asked us to make it another day. But Gerald wanted her downstairs, she was being rude to his guests to absent herself for such a long time.

'Long time!' cried Mary angrily, 'We've only been here half-an-hour. Don't he reckon you should have friends of your own who can pop in without warning? What's he think, we got the plague or something? Come on, Margaret, let's go somewhere more suited to our station in life.'

Turning to Rose, Mary added, sarcastically, 'Is it all right if we leave by the front door? I don't suppose Mrs Rush would mind if we went through her kitchen. Maybe we could stop and have a chat with her; or would *Master* Gerald object to us even being below stairs.'

Poor Rose was nearly in tears as she showed us out and I was sorry that Mary had upset her. After all, we had arrived unexpectedly and it wasn't Rose's fault that she couldn't entertain us. As we walked down the drive, Mary was still fulminating about our reception:

'Never again, Margaret, never again. All this long journey just to be shown the door. What's the matter with us that we have to be poked in some corner because her guests mustn't see us? What if they did? Who are they anyway? They're not real gentry, they've made their money in business. Why couldn't we meet them?'

'We couldn't meet them, Mary, because we were domestic servants in Gerald's house and he knows it. We could never be on an equal footing. Besides, if all the females were as well-dressed as Rose, we'd have looked a bit conspicuous in our outfits. I wouldn't have wanted to mix with them. In any case, Mary, this long journey cost us nothing; Mr Davies drove us here. What I'd like to know is, what are we going to do now? It'll be two hours before he comes to pick us up. Two hours stuck here with nothing to do.'

That two hours was about the most tedious I'd ever spent; it seemed more like four hours. We didn't dare stray too far in case we lost our way. By the time Mr Davies arrived we were fed up with the country sights, the weather and even with our own company; though when he asked if we'd enjoyed ourselves, we looked at each other and started to laugh. As he'd been kind enough to take us out we felt that we should explain the situation to him; get an outsider's opinion of our welcome, or lack of it.

We'd travelled nearly five miles before Mr Davies spoke – I thought he'd forgotten what we'd told him. Then, after some hemming and hawing he said, sagely, 'Ah! It never does to marry out of one's station. My wife's sister-in-law's cousin, over to Ruthin, was as strict a chapel-goer as you'd be likely to meet in the whole of Denbighshire. She was a good-looking lass but a bit simple like, could hardly read or write. She was still not married at twenty-eight; though mind you, she'd had her chances. But she couldn't seem to fancy any of the local lads. Old Farmer Hyde would have given his eye teeth to get Molly; never mind she couldn't read, she could do the work of two women. He'd had a nice farm, money and all, but Molly said she'd as soon bed down with Ambrose – that was Farmer Hyde's prize pig. And then, who do you think she went off with? You'd never believe.'

We answered that we'd no idea and endeavoured to give the impression that we were consumed with curioisity to know with whom his wife's sister-in-law's cousin, Molly, had departed.

'Well, one day,' said Mr Davies dramatically, 'a circus came to Ruthin, and Molly couldn't do a thing for excitement over this circus; she'd never seen the like. She went every night and sat bang in the front row. The circus stayed a week and when it was gone, so was Molly. She left a note saying that she and Carlo – the elephant trainer – were going to be married. And Carlo was teaching her to ride on the elephants. To think,' he added, 'that Molly, who could have been Mrs Hyde, is now riding around on the back of an elephant, and at her age too. As I said, it never does to marry out of your station.'

Mary and I kept our sentiments to ourselves and merely murmured agreement.

As though not enough had gone wrong, when I got back I found sixteen-year-old Bessie weeping copiously because the butcher boy hadn't turned up to meet her and she was sure he'd found another girl. Having so recently lost my own boyfriend, I felt sympathy for Bessie; though, as I told her, she was only sixteen and had plenty of time to find herself another beau. But she was inconsolable and was going to give in her notice as she couldn't face seeing the butcher boy again. She wasn't a very competent kitchenmaid, but I didn't want to work with a stranger so I told her not to worry; I'd open the door to him.

Mr Kite looked disapproving as he remarked that, when he was young, servants had to work too hard to have the time, or inclination for imagining themselves in love. But then I don't suppose he'd ever felt desire and passion. Although he occasionally said that all a man needed in life was comfort and love, I think he visualised a maternal kind. I'm sure that the other kind would have frightened him to death.

21

Shortly after our employers return from Holland, an incident occurred that almost led to the butler and I giving in our notice, though for different reasons. Madam was pleased with the results of our spring-cleaning – though none of us received any pecuniary reward for our hard work. I expect Madam knew we had not worked in the evenings, so the freedom was our reward. Even in as good a situation as ours, it was considered quite the normal thing that servants should rise early in the morning and be on call at any time up to an hour before midnight; even later than that if there were guests in the house. The incident referred to was that Mr Van Lievden had invited two Russian emigrés – man and wife who lived in Paris – to be his guests for a few weeks. The man was a Count Kylev, and on the day that they arrived the butler came down to tell us that they looked just the same as we did. I think Mr Kite expected to see the Count wearing a shirt outside his trousers and the trouser legs tucked into high boots. The following morning Madam asked me if I knew any Russian cooking, and I promptly answered that I had absolutely no idea what kind of food they ate in Russia, let alone knowing how to cook it. I had gone through my 1887 edition of Mrs Beeton, but the only recipe I could find there was Russian salad. This involved making an aspic jelly as a border mould, and filling the centre with cold flaked turbot, anchovies, olives and mayon-naise. When I showed the recipe to Madam she said that there was nothing typically Russian about it, and asked if I would let Count Kylov come down into the kitchen occasionally to make a Russian dish, as he was a good cook. I should have had the sense to be cautious in agreeing but, not knowing what it entailed and feeling that it would be an unusual and exciting event to have a Russian count in my kitchen, I said that I didn't mind. Two mornings later he came down to make bortsch, a soup I'd never heard of then, and things called viziga patties, to be served with the soup. My kitchen was occupied by him the entire morning while I was trying to cook the lunch for upstairs and dinner for us, and the chaos on my kitchen table was indescribable. There wasn't even any pleasure in having him there, for the Count, a man about fifty years old, never once smiled; and apart from saying good morning to me, the only other words he spoke were to ask for various utensils. He also complained to Madam that bortsch couldn't be made properly with ordinary beetroot; in his native Russia they used kvass – whatever that was. The viziga he'd bought in Paris; I had to soak it overnight, then it was cooked in boiling salted water until soft. It looked like boiled tapioca – and was about as thick. The work involved in making these patties hardly seemed worth the bother. This tapioca stuff had to be mixed with chopped hard-boiled eggs and onions. Then Count Kylov made some special pastry, using plain flour, milk, egg yolks and yeast. I particularly remember the yeast because he had to wait for the dough to rise, which was why it took so long to make the stuff. Then it had to be rolled out, cut into small round pieces, a spoonful of the viziga mixture put on one half and the other half turned over it to make a patty. Then the patties had to be baked in the oven. All that work and messing around just to eat them as an *accompaniment*! It was never worth the effort. When the Count finally left my kitchen, he never even said thank you. Bessie complained about the mounds of washing-up he'd made and I felt equally disgruntled about the mess on my kitchen table. The following morning, when Madam came down to give the orders for the day, she said that the soup and the viziga patties were delicious, didn't I think so? I didn't, but I thought it politic to agree with her in case she imagined I was envious because I couldn't have made them myself.

At dinner that same evening, while the butler was serving the famous soup and patties, the talk was all about how different things had been in Russia before the revolution, and what a lavish household the Count and Countess had run in those days. Now I look back it was really very funny, for Mr Kite, our normally very placid butler, came into my kitchen between each course to express his annoyance at the conversation going on upstairs. After he and Norma had served the first course, Mr Kite said, 'Would you credit it, Cook, that Russian spoke about his grandfather's serfs. Not servants, mark you, Cook, but serfs. You know what they are don't you? Little better than slaves.' Then, after he'd served the jugged hare, he came in again, still complaining:

'Cook, I don't wonder that they had a revolution in Russia if all the wealthy people were like that man. After I'd served the salmon with your lovely mayonnaise sauce, all he said was that he'd give Madam a recipe for salmon cooked in bouillon, and when he tasted the jugged hare he said that in Russia they cooked it with red wine instead of port. What kind of a guest is that to criticise the food? Mr Van Lievden took no notice, but Madam didn't look too pleased, I can tell you, Cook. And the way he treated Norma and me, just as though we weren't real flesh and blood. Well, we've never had serfs in this country and I very nearly told him so.'

Of course Mr Kite's remark was not to be taken seriously. In the privacy of our servants' hall we all, at one time or another – if we thought we'd been 'put upon' – avowed we'd say this or that to Sir or Madam, but it was just a way of letting off steam. So when that same evening Mr Kite stated pontifically what he would say to the Count, we all knew it was just bravado, he never would – not unless he wanted instant dismissal. Odette, unusually for her, actually sympathised with our butler, saying that she disliked the Russians; all the so-called aristocracy were arrogant and overbearing. At her age, and never having worked for a Russian family, how could she know what they were like? Odette also disliked the Dutch and wasn't keen on the English; it seemed to me that she considered the French only were the right kind of people. Young Norma, the parlourmaid, had taken little notice or interest in what had been discussed above stairs; I think she was too bemused by waiting on a real live count and countess.

Count Kylov came down again two days later to make another dish which I'd never heard of. It was beef stroganoff. His recipe required two pounds of fillet beef, sour cream, butter, mushrooms, onion, Worcester sauce and seasoning. It took some time to make, but I must admit the finished result was extremely good. I really didn't mind the work this entailed in clearing-up after him; but what I did object to was the haughty and high-handed manner in which he asked for things. He ordered me about as though I was some menial doing the lowest kind of job – instead of a skilled cook with a kitchenmaid to help. Towards the end I was so choked with fury that I didn't even call him Sir; I just got what he asked for and said nothing. At our midday dinner, the butler and I decided we'd had enough. Mr Kite was even more unnerved than I was, because the Count expected to be valeted. The only personal service that our butler had to do for Mr Van Lievden was to brush his suits, Mr Van Lievden preferred to look after himself. Now here was this Russian ringing his bedroom bell at any time in the evening and expecting the butler to wait on him.

'Who does he think I am?' Mr Kite exclaimed, indignantly, 'one of his peasants, one of the serfs his grandfather used to own, body and soul?'

'No, no, Mr Kite,' said Odette, soothingly, 'not a peasant, more like a kulak.'

But as our butler had no knowledge of kulaks, and was determined not to ask Odette, he wasn't soothed.

Both Elsie, and Ada, the under-housemaid, said that the

Countess was a very nice person indeed. She had taken a personal interest in them, and expressed commiseration at Elsie's long engagement – unaware that Elsie didn't really mind. I thought then that the Countess must assume Englishmen to be very cold-blooded if Elsie's Jack could wait seven years for her; though personally, I doubted Jack would be a very ardent husband anyway, well, ardent in the physical sense. Being so accustomed to dealing with cows, he'd probably pat Elsie's flanks and say, 'Come along, old gal, get over there'.

My friends, Gladys and Mary, came to tea that day so naturally they had to hear about our visitors; especially from Mr Kite, who rather liked Gladys, though he was often shocked at her rather crude remarks. Gladys was one of those people who, whenever you told her some incident about a particular person or mentioned that you'd once visited a certain place, she knew somebody exactly the same; and if she had never visited the place herself, she always knew somebody who had. So Gladys proceeded to tell us that her sister-in-law had a friend, Clara, who'd married a Russian, and what a grief he'd turned out to be. I thought it odd that Gladys, whom I'd known for some considerable time, had never before mentioned this Alexander Chakmar – a name like that wouldn't be easy to forget.

'Clara met Alex one Saturday evening at the Palais de Dance,' said Gladys, 'and she was up in the clouds when he offered to escort her home; such a good-looking chap as he was didn't often come her way, as Clara's a bit on the plain side. Well, to be honest, her figure's not so bad but her face is a bit puddeny. Mind you, Clara's not like us, she never left school until she was sixteen. She can take shorthand and type so she works in an office. Lucky for her that she can earn her living, for that Alex is bone idle. He earns about a couple of pounds a week entertaining pub customers by a bit of singing and doing imitations – he does Maurice Chevalier. He's as vain as a turkey-cock and tries to make out that he's a somebody; says that his ancestors came from the Steppes – whatever they are. I ask you, how would that Alex know? He was born in this country.'

'There must be more to him than you know of, Gladys,' I said, 'otherwise Clara wouldn't have married him, surely?'

'Well, Margaret,' and Gladys giggled madly, 'there's only one thing that he works overtime at and that's why Clara's been in the family way three times in as many years. If it was me, I'd soon tell him where he got off. In fact,' added Gladys, smiling at our butler, 'I'd darn well make sure that he never "got on".'

Poor Mr Kite looked scandalised as well he might. Though he'd never experienced 'le grande passion' himself, it was to be presumed that he was aware of the mechanics involved. With the others, I laughed at Gladys's story – she was my friend – but really I failed to see the connection between our Russian visitors and Clara's Alex. His shortcomings in the matrimonial stakes were not exclusive to his Russian ancestry; plenty of Englishmen have shattered love's young dream.

Later on that day, Mr Kite asked me if I really intended to tell Madam that I didn't want Count Kylov in my kitchen.

'Yes, Mr Kite, I shall mention it. It's no part of my job to have one of the guests below stairs. I take orders only from Mrs Van Lievden, she pays me.'

'Well, I'll not stand for it either, Cook. I've been in the best service, I can get another job at any time. Just you read this reference from one of my situations. The gentleman wrote it for me just before he went abroad. With a reference like that, I don't need to stay in a place where I'm put upon.'

I wasn't so much interested in reading the reference as I was amused to discover what his Christian names were: Algernon Rufus. Somehow Mr Kite didn't look like an Algernon Rufus. With initials, ARK, I wondered if he'd been known as Noah's Ark at school; though as Mr Kite wasn't noted for a sense of humour, I decided not to ask.

'What do you think of that, Cook? Doesn't that show you I know my job? I started at the bottom and worked my way to the top. Why, I could have gone to America with one of my gentlemen. And he told me that he was sure his American friends would try to bribe me with offers of much higher wages to get a perfect English butler. Good menservants are worth their weight in gold over there. Not that I need to leave England to find another post,' Mr Kite added, very much on his dignity. 'Employers don't mind paying the tax if they can get a good manservant.'

I felt slightly peeved that he should put such stress on the value of butlers and menservants in general, as opposed to us women – after all, I thought, hadn't somebody once written: 'We may live without friends; we may live without books; but civilised man cannot live without cooks'. I quoted this to Mr Kite, adding, perhaps with some malice, that the only verse I knew about butlers was from Hilaire Belloc; 'In my opinion Butlers ought to know their place, and not to play The Old Retainer night and day'. In any case it wasn't strictly true that employers didn't mind paying the tax on menservants. I used to read the newspapers that came down from upstairs, especially the readers' letters in *The Times*. I had visions of writing to the paper and getting a letter published; though on what subject, I'd no idea. But in some of the letters, employers were complaining about having to pay this domestic tax. Considering that it was only 15/-, I couldn't imagine why they made such a fuss. To people who could afford a large staff of domestic servants, what was an extra 15/-?

As it transpired, neither the butler nor I need have worried about 'speaking to Madam'. Before we had a chance to complain, the Russian visitors had departed. Naturally, none of us servants were told the reason why their visit had been cut short.

22

Two days elapsed before I saw Mrs Van Lievden, for Odette gave me a message that Madam was indisposed and I was to plan the menus; she was sure I could cope. It was on the second day of Madam's indisposition that the Count and Countess left the house. None of us regretted *his* departure, though he did provide me with an original topic of conversation; after all, not every cook can talk about the count in her kitchen – what a good title for a book. When speaking about his culinary achievements in my kitchen, I naturally always omitted to mention that Count Kylov spoke to me only when he required some kitchen utensil – it would have detracted from my glory. Working below stairs, I'd never spoke to the Countess, but Odette and Elsie agreed that she was a very sweet person; quiet, timid and apparently much in awe of her husband, who frequently spoke to her in a harsh manner.

The following morning, Mrs Van Lievden came down as usual to give the orders for the day. Now although the servants were interested in, and discussed every facet of life above stairs – or what little we knew of it – this interest was certainly not reciprocated. Madam was concerned to know that her servants had everything they needed in the way of uniforms, household equipment, comfortable bedrooms and servants' hall, but that was the extent of her interest in us as persons. But this morning, for the first and only time, Mrs Van Lievden spoke to me of matters not appertaining to working out the menu. She asked if Count Kylov had been rude to me or to Mr Kite; and she went on to explain that the Count had suffered great hardships in that he had lost his beautiful home, money and possessions – it certainly hadn't made him feel compassion for those who'd never had those assets in the first place, I thought. Madam seemed concerned that I should understand how hard life was for the Russian emigrés, now that the Bolshevists had driven them from their own country.

'But of course, Cook,' she said, 'you were far too young to remember anything about the Russian Revolution of 1917. I'm sure you are not in the least interested in Russia, and there's no reason why you should be.'

'I do know something about pre-revolution Russia, Madam. I borrowed Tolstoy's *War and Peace* from our public library, and I've also read *The Possessed* by Dostoievsky, and a volume of short stories by Anton Chekhov. I enjoyed reading the books, Madam.'

Madam was so taken aback that she could only utter, and somewhat feebly, 'Did you, Cook?'

Everything was just settling down into the usual routine when Bessie, the kitchenmaid, decided to give in her notice. Not only was she still lamenting the faithlessness of the butcher-boy, but she'd discovered she didn't like being a kitchenmaid. The work was too hard; she'd get a place as an under-housemaid. It was my opinion, and the butcher's also that in comparison with what we had to do when we started in domestic service, Bessie was in clover. She didn't have to get up in the morning until six-thirty, and a whole hour later on Sundays, and she'd no kitchen range to light, just an Ideal boiler to rake out. In my first job, there was a list of the kitchenmaid's duties pinned on to the dresser, and what I had to do before eight o'clock: RISE AT 5.30AM, ON SUNDAYS 6.00AM. LIGHT THE RANGE, CLEAN THE FLUES, POLISH THE RANGE AND EMERY-PAPER THE FENDER AND FIRE-IRONS. CLEAN THE BRASS ON THE FRONT DOOR, THE TILES IN THE FRONT HALL AND HEARTHSTONE THE STEPS.

POLISH THE BOOTS AND SHOES FOR THE FOUR PERSONS ABOVE STAIRS, LAY UP THE SERVANTS' BREAKFAST AND SET OUT THE KITCHEN TABLE WITH ALL THAT THE COOK WILL NEED. When I first saw this list my mind boggled. I thought that I'd never be able to do it all in the time. But I managed. Mr Kite and I agreed that we didn't know what the younger generation were coming to – which is of course, precisely what people say today.

Then it was time for Odette to go back to France. I would miss her, but she wasn't sorry to be leaving England, comparing it unfavourably with her native Provençe. I pointed out that she barely knew England; living in London, with a few odd weeks in Bath, Harrogate and Edinburgh, she was hardly familiar with our country. We had lovely old towns and villages that Odette had never heard of, much less seen. But then she didn't like Englishmen; for either they were too formal, stand-offish, cold as fish – and cod-like too; or they were as crude in their methods of showing affection as a gorilla in the zoo. Leaping to the defence of our males, especially as I was still looking for a permanent beau, I retaliated by saying that Raoul, the Frenchman I'd met at the Palais de Dance, was a pretty poor specimen of humanity. I didn't so much mind that he was a second-rate dancer, for I was no twinkle-toes; what I did mind was his ineffable conceit in thinking that his ridiculous gyrations on the dance floor made him a marvellous partner. Furthermore, his ideas about kissing were certainly not mine. I strongly objected to being almost swallowed when we said goodnight. Odette explained that Raoul was probably out to prove a Frenchman was more passionate than a cold Englishman. He probably was, but I very soon told him to prove it with some other girl; it wasn't passion I was looking for, it was marriage lines.

Rose wrote to Mary and me to say that her parents were thinking of doing the same as Uncle Fred in coming to London to work. The world wide Great Depression was still throwing more and more people out of work; now Rose's father had lost his job in the mill. Uncle Fred had managed to get work as a lift attendant; the hours were long and the wages small, but it was better than being on the dole. Rose wanted Mary and me to look for a small flat suitable for her ma and pa. Her letter was full of the usual complaints about her husband. Gerald had refused to have ma and pa staying at Greenlands, giving as a reason that her pa disliked him and there would be rows – too true, said Mary. Gerald had offered to pay the rent of a flat, but she, Rose, knew that her pa would flatly refuse to accept charity. Pa's temper had never been mild at the best of times it was positively dreadful now that he was out of work. That being so, I couldn't see Mary and me calling on her parents as we had called on Uncle Fred. As I remarked to Mary, Shakespeare's banished Duke may have thought, 'sweet are the uses of adversity', but evidently adversity hadn't sweetened Rose's pa.

After the fiasco of our visit to Greenlands, Mary still felt some animosity towards Rose. She said, satirically, 'Margaret, isn't it just like Rose to expect us to wear ourselves out walking around London to find a flat for her parents! Could you see her doing the same for us? Notice too, that she hasn't enclosed any money so that we could get around in comfort by having a taxi. Oh no! A bus is good enough for us. And why should we give up our free time? I could think of a lot of things I'd rather do. Besides, I start my new job next week and I've some shopping to do. I think I'm going to like this new place. There's only four above stairs; no children, thank heaven, and they don't have coal fires in the bedrooms, not even for guests. Not that I'd have to lug coal-scuttles up the stairs, there's an under-housemaid to do that. I have to provide my own uniform and caps, but I'm getting £40 a year. And the butler's such a nice-looking man; young too, I bet he's only about thirty-five.'

'Now then, Mary, don't start off the job with romantic ideas about the menservants. Remember what a disaster that Alf turned out to be – ' But here Mary interrupted to say that Alf was never a manservant, it was just an extra job for him.

'Maybe so, but if the butler is young and goodlooking, he's either engaged or married. If he isn't, considering all the females below stairs, it must be that he doesn't like women.'

'Oh, Margaret! Why do you have to be such a wet blanket? It

could well be that he hasn't found the right woman yet. Besides, not all men rush into matrimony in their twenties.'

'Well, Mary, in my opinion, any reasonably good-looking man in his thirties, who's still single, will have very little enthusiasm for walking up the aisle with a bride. Besides, you surely wouldn't want to marry a butler and be in service for the rest of your life?'

A butler doesn't have to stay in service, does he? He can get another kind of job.'

'What! with a million and a half unemployed? What would he do? He'd look fine in the dole queue when they asked him what kind of work could he do! He'd have to say, "I can buttle".'

Beating Mary in an argument was a bit pointless when we were spending some hours together, for generally it took her time to recover her equanimity. But now she just laughed, saying, 'we've got time to dash in the pub for a quick one before we start flat-hunting.' The barman, who was Welsh and a friend of ours, asked us where we were off to.

'We're looking for a small flat, or rooms of some kind, Morgan. Do you know of anything round this way?'

'Well, I never, sweethearts. Is it that you are going to set up home together now? What a waste of good material.'

Mary and I blushed a fiery red. We thought that he meant were we setting up a brothel. We knew only of men like that; probably what he meant was, were we a couple of lesbians.

23

As a way of spending a pleasant afternoon, I wouldn't advocate hunting for accommodation. It was much worse a few years later when I had a family and needed rooms, but even now Mary and I had a wearisome time. We'd bought the local newspapers of Kensington, Notting Hill Gate and Earl's Court, and we started off fairly confident of finding a suitable place.

At the first house, in Earl's Court, the door was opened by a young man whose fair curly hair and high-pitched voice made it obvious where his sexual preferences lay. He smiled at us, saying, 'Come in, my dears, come in, I'll show you the rooms.'

We explained that it wasn't for ourselves we were seeking accommodation, and again he gave us a sweet smile.

'What a pity, my dears, what a pity. I do like to have young people around me.'

He repeated most of his remarks; whether to emphasise or prolong the conversation, we'd no idea. The house was very clean but it was all furnished accommodation so wouldn't do for Rose's parents. Her ma would never be parted from her green plush chairs and china dogs. The amicable young proprietor said that he let furnished rooms because he simply loved to be surrounded by his own things.

'My dears, you've no idea. Once, just as a favour, I did let a tenant bring her own things. They were simply hideous, simply hideous; gave me a headache just to look at them.'

'But, Mr Martin, if you let unfurnished rooms, you didn't have to go into the rooms.'

'Ah, my dears, you don't understand. Just to know such things were in my house upset me, yes upset me. I must have my own things.'

I had an hilarious vision of him sitting with Rose's ma and pa surrounded by the green plush chairs and green plush over-mantel, complete with china dogs. He'd have had the headache of all time. He made tea for us and introduced us to his 'friend', Aubrey, a hefty six-foot man. As Mary said, no doubt Aubrey was the 'chucker-out' of undesirable tenants. In those days it was possible for a landlord to get rid of them.

Next on the list was a house in Notting Hill Gate where the land-lady, in hair curlers and wearing a sacklike garment – on which it was possible, to discern the remains of many meals – was extremely gar-rulous. She showed us the dark, empty and cavernous basement flat, which stank of countless previous cave-dwellers; perhaps the midden was in the yard. Oh, yes, she liked people from the North. Her late husband had come from Yorkshire, as hard-working a man as you'd hope to find though suffering something cruel with his 'waterworks'. He had to hop in and out of bed all night, they could never get down to a bit of the 'you know what'. It carried him off eventually; thank gawd she had no kids to bring up.

What with the smell of the basement and the torrent of words, Mary and I were thankful to get out into the fresh air. We col-lected particulars of some half-dozen more or less suitable places, and I suggested to Mary that perhaps we should telephone Rose and give her the information.

'What! at our expense?' Mary exclaimed, 'you must be mad. It'll cost us a packet and we'd never get our money back. No, send it through the post.'

Our chauffeur's wife had invited us to supper in their mews flat; and as I was short of money – it being still a few days to go before my month's wages – we called on Mrs Davies as early as etiquette allowed. The supper was a delicious beef stew, which Mrs Davies said she'd made from shin of beef. At the time I doubted her, for in service I used shin of beef only to make beef tea, and I then threw away the meat. It was only about sixpence a pound then. Off duty, Mr Davies was a very entertaining man, with a fund of stories about his childhood in Glamorgan. Every midsummer his grand-parents had made mead, ready for a grand gathering of the Davies clan at Christmas, and his mother had cooked a ham, with cider, and made dumplings to go with it – made not with ordinary flour, but with oatmeal.

Mrs Gwyneth Davies made us a 'special' welsh rarebit; she said the recipe had been given to her by her grandmother, who'd worked as a cook in Glamorgan.

'Grandmother worked for a very wealthy ironmaster,' said Gwyneth Davies, 'and she was always telling me that being in ser-vice then was the natural thing, one wasn't looked down on, not like now. Grandmother said that her employer, John Lewis, had made his money the hard way. He'd started in the iron-works when he was only ten years old, and sweated fourteen hours a day. Grandmother said that her employer, Mrs Lewis, would come into the kitchen and sit down – just as we are sitting here – and she'd say to Grand-mother, "Come on, my gel, what are we eating today?", just as though Grandma was one of them. Can you imagine Mrs Van Lievden do-ing that?'

Well, no, I couldn't, thank goodness. Nothing would induce me to work for a lady who made herself at home in my kitchen and said 'gel, what are we eating today?'

There was much eating going on, as Mr Van Lievden's mother and two aunts from Schiedam were staying in the house. Madam had asked Mr Kite and me if we minded the guests inspecting the below stairs, as kitchens in Holland were very different from those in England. Our butler wasn't very pleased, complaining to me that it was not the done thing for employers to poke their noses into our departments. In his usual prim manner, he said:

'I have been in service many more years than you, Cook; and, believe me, I've always found it best to stick to correct procedures: they have their domain and we have ours. Would we ever ask them if we could show our relatives the upstairs because it was different from below? Of course we wouldn't.'

'Well, Mr Kite, it does happen to be their house. Presumably they are entitled to be in any part of it on occasions. What have we got to worry about? There's nothing in my kitchen or scullery that I don't want seen by them above stairs.'

'That's not it, Cook, it's the principle of the thing.'

Muttering to myself about where he could stuff his principles, I made sure that Bessie had cleaned and polished everything. Though now that she was leaving, Bessie had suddenly become a quick and willing worker. Like all of us in service, she was thinking about her reference for the next place.

Mr Van Lievden's mother and aunts, judging by their substantial girth, looked as though the consuming of large quantities of food was one of their chief occupations. And so it proved; for during the next two weeks I cooked vast quantities. For breakfast, dishes of porridge, sausages, bacon and eggs, kippers and kedgeree went upstairs full and came down empty. There were three-course lunches and six-course dinners. I marvelled that anybody – especially people who didn't work – could consume such gargantuan meals. One evening we had a dinner party for eighteen people. A woman came in to help with the washing up, and a special iced-pudding was ordered from an outside caterer. I prepared a clear soup; salmon maître d'hôtel; roast quails – silly little birds I thought them, a few mouthfuls and they were eaten – and a main course of roast sirloin served with cauliflower au gratin, glazed carrots, petit pois and duchesse potatoes. The savoury was simple, just cheese straws. I remember that one of the guests was a vegetarian so I had the bother of cooking her a baked aubergine instead of the quails, and haricot bean croquettes instead of roast sirloin. I grumbled to Mr Kite that vegetarians should stay at home but, although he murmured a word of sympathy, I could tell he wasn't interested. His interests lay elsewhere that evening; Mr Kite was in his element. A retired butler had been engaged to help wait at table, and Mr Kite was surprised and gratified to discover that this Mr Penny had been the butler while our Mr Kite was a first footman. Now the positions were reversed and Mr Kite was in charge. True, he hadn't a footman under him, but he had Norma and an ex-butler – a staff of three in the butler's pantry!

It was around eleven o'clock before we could sit down to our supper of cold ham, potatoes and salad, followed by blackcurrant tart with cream. Off duty, Mr Penny was very good company. He and Mr Kite were soon deep in reminiscences of Lord – who shall be nameless – with a handsome wife and five children who, not content with that, had another 'lady' and two more children in the same town. And there was the Honourable Charles, who'd seduced the housemaid and got his come-uppance when the girl's father and brother set on him in the street and gave him a black eye and a bloody nose.

I had no such colourful tit-bits to contribute to the conversation, but I made them all laugh with an account of the time I'd gone into Mrs Bishop's bathroom for the day's orders and found a naked man standing in the bath; the sight was a terrible shock to me.

'Dear dear, Cook,' laughed Mr Penny, 'it was probably only the loofah you saw; in the steamy atmosphere, outlines get blurred. You know, it reminds me of the time when I was young. After five years as second, then first footman, I'd taken my first place as a butler. You wouldn't think, to see me now, that I used to be quite a good-looking chap.'

'Oh, Mr Penny,' we chorused, 'you're still a fine-looking man, do go on with your story.'

'Well, by the time I'd been there three months, I could tell that the lady of the house had taken quite a shine to me. Big-head that I was, I felt flattered. Although Madam must have been ten years older than me, she was still a pretty woman. I'm telling you, it was Penny this and Penny that, with a sweet smile and a helpless look, from the time her husband left the house in the morning until he returned about six o'clock.'

'What happened, Mr Penny?'

'I'm coming to that. One afternoon, I was soaking myself in a lovely hot bath – our bathroom was in the basement. I hadn't bothered to lock the door; there was no need, for Cook was having her afternoon nap, the housemaid upstairs was sorting out the linen cupboard and the tweeny was out. You'll never believe the next bit, but it's as true as I'm sitting here. There I am in the bath, rubbing my heels with pumice stone – a butler needs to take care of his feet – when suddenly, the bathroom door opens and Madam comes in. I was fit to die with shock, I can tell you; no female has ever seen me unclothed since the time I told my mother I was old enough to bath myself. "Oh, Penny", she said, with such a look on her face that you'd have thought she was going to eat me – and she'd taken too much of the brandy after lunch – "do let me wash your back. Lovely Penny, you're not a penny, you're worth your weight in gold". And she put her hands right in the water saying, "Let me find the soap". It wasn't the soap she was feeling for, that I did know. The shameless woman!'

Amid the general laughter, I asked what happened after that.

'Well, Cook, I practically threw Madam out, got dressed and left the house. It wasn't possible to stay as a butler for such a Jezebel. It's true that her husband was an elderly man, probably Madam married him for his money. Well she'd got that, but it didn't buy me.'

'But, Mr Penny how did you manage about the reference for your next place?'

'I forged one. Said that my employers had gone to America and left me this written reference. They were satisfied, took me on and I stayed with them for five years. And here I am, like Mr Kite, still a bachelor but fond of the ladies.'

'We were all sorry when the taxi came to take Mr Penny home. I'd hoped that Mr Kite would invite him to call one afternoon and have tea with us, but I expect he was rather envious of the ex-butler, who had obviously led a more interesting life than Kite had.

It was indeed a pleasant surprise when our Dutch guests thanked us personally for all the extra work – and they tipped us well. As Elsie remarked, we were so lucky. We might have been servants in a house – and there were many such – where those above stairs, employers and guests alike, hardly recognised us as human beings.

Elsie had another pleasant surprise when her fiancé suddenly presented himself at the basement door. From Elsie's description of Jack, and the fact that, like Jacob for his Rachel, he had been courting Elsie for seven years, I'd visualised him looking beefy, stolid and quite out of place in a city. Instead, there he was, six-feet tall, slim, brown eyes and curly hair, wearing as smart a suit as any city beau. I couldn't imagine how Elsie had been content to see her Jack just once a month, apart from holidays, year after year. If he had been my boyfriend, I'd have been afraid of some other girl offering consolation during my absence. But perhaps down on the farm there weren't many unattached girls around. Jack had come with the good news that he'd been made head stockman. The job paid higher wages and included a house, so there was no reason why he and Elsie should wait any longer to be married. Elsie agreed to give in her notice, but she wasn't noticeably overwhelmed with excitement – as I would have been.

The next morning, I had the temerity to reproach Elsie for her lukewarm reception of Jack's good fortune, and Elsie almost wept as she moaned. 'I know, Cook, I know. But I don't really want to be married. I like being in service, especially this place. I don't want to lose my independence.'

'Independence Elsie! What independence? What kind of independence have we got, even here? How can any woman be independent when she can't earn enough money to provide a decent living and save for her old age. Sure, they've given us the vote – though even then they had to denigrate it by calling it "the flapper vote" – but what good does the vote do us, especially in service? Have we any more rights? It's true that this is a good place to work in, but if we demanded to be called "Miss" instead of our surnames; if we insisted that we should be free after nine o'clock at night, how long do you think we'd be here? And how would we get another job? If we told a prospective employer that we were dismissed because we insisted that work, starting at seven o'clock in the morning, should end by nine o'clock at night, d'you think we'd be engaged as servants? Not on your life we wouldn't. The very idea of servants wanting regular hours!'

Elsie was so bemused with this expatiation on independence and the thought of giving in her notice, that she was late with Madam's tea-tray in the bedroom. She was reprimanded for this, and in turn reprimanded Ada the under-housemaid for not reminding her about the time. So, what with poor Ada weeping, Elsie peeved because she'd promised Jack that she'd give in her notice, and the butler looking aloof and disapproving, the morning was a disaster.

I, too, wanted to be independent; but with no money or social standing it would not be possible to achieve independence by eschewing men. As my mother told me, it was men who bitterly opposed giving women the vote; men who still jealously guarded all the male priviliges appertaining to work and social life. The very idea that a woman wanted a life free from dependence on a man, it would have infuriated the male ego to such an extent that they would have closed ranks against her. I was determined to marry and achieve an equal partnership. Although I would probably still have little money, I intended to have, in my marriage, as much freedom as the male had always had by inalienable right.

Lack of money, with the approach of old age and inability to work, was a constant anxiety to domestics. With no home of their own and parents gone, what would become of them? The government pension was barely enough to pay rent for a room, let alone provide food. A few servants, after years of faithful service, were rewarded with a small pension; but the majority could expect, and got, nothing.

Mrs Lawton, Rose's mother, had for years corresponded with her old employer, Mrs Paine, But when Madam died, all she left to Mrs

Lawton was two china spotted dogs. As an addition to the green plush over-mantel they may have been welcome, but they certainly did nothing to ease the financial situation. Rose told Mary and me that her father had been so incensed at the arrival of the canine pair – after his years of listening to Mrs Lawton's 'dear Madam this and dear Madam that' – that he'd threatened to smash them and send back the pieces to dear madam's son.

Rose's father, despairing of getting back his job in the mill, was moving to London. Mary and I had found them a place in Kensington; and though only three rooms in a semi-basement, they would have their own entrance and not have to share the lavatory. Mary and I, with Rose, had spent all one afternoon and evening cleaning the place in preparation for her mother's arrival. Her father would follow a week later.

24

Now that her parents were coming down from Manchester to live in London, Mary and I were seeing Rose more often. When part of the furniture arrived, we had been to the rooms to arrange it, and Mr Davies had laid the linoleum in the kitchen. Rose was very much changed from the parlourmaid we had known at Mrs Wardham's. Not in looks, for she was still very attractive, but in disposition. As a domestic servant she had been a quiet girl; a bit dull perhaps, but always ready to smile and laugh at a joke. Now she had a permanently discontented look, and when Mary and I were with her Rose never ceased to complain about her husband's lack of consideration.

Rose asked me to be with her when she met her mother at the station one Sunday evening. Mrs Lawton still looked as dour, stern and upright as when I'd met her in Manchester, determined neither to ask for sympathy nor receive it. Rose was apprehensive, wondering what her ma would say when she saw the semi-basement rooms and our arrangement of the furniture. Though laden with two heavy suitcases, her mother flatly refused to let us get a taxi – she was obviously determined to be a martyr – so we had to struggle onto a bus. The bus conductor, with typical cockney humour said, as he helped us with the cases:

'Hello, girls, doing a moonlight flit, then?' In the face of her mother's sour and disapproving look, Rose didn't dare to laugh, but I had no such inhibitions:

'No, mate, I'm off to Gretna Green. My mum's coming with me to make sure I get spliced.'

When we got to the house, Rose started trying to explain to her mother that Gerald would have willingly paid the rent for a proper flat; but her ma interrupted, saying fiercely, 'Your pa won't accept charity, not from your husband or anybody else. We've always paid our way, never owed anybody a penny and we never will, we'd sooner starve.'

I'm sure she would have, too. Rose had stocked the kitchen cupboard with food and stores, put a couple of hundredweight of coal in the cellar under the stairs and generously fed the gas meter; while Mary and I had cleaned and polished. Her mother said not a word about all these preparations for her comfort but sat in grim silence while we made a pot of tea. Rose was dressed as plainly as possible, and she now lapsed into an even stronger northern accent than she generally used – in order to make her mother feel at home, I supposed.

Suddenly Mrs Lawton said, 'Where's Victoria Helen, then? Why haven't you brought her with you? We haven't seen her for six months. I suppose we're not high-class enough, is that it?'

'You know it's not like that, Ma. How could I bring her at this time of night? She goes to bed at six o'clock. I'll bring her over in a day or two, when you're settled in.'

'If that husband of yours will let his child mix with the likes of us. I suppose Madam is still the doting grandmother.'

I rashly intervened to say that she wasn't Madam now, she was Rose's mother-in-law.

'She's still Madam to me, and always will be. I don't hold with people marrying out of their class, it never works out right. Stands to reason it can't when one of the parties is gentry and the other's working class; they don't mix. Look at our Rose here, she's not happy married to one of them above stairs. Her husband's always trying to make her over, make her into what he calls a lady. Our Rose doesn't need to be like one of them, why should she be? Gerald knew what she was when he married her, just a simple north country lass. Why should he expect her to change her speech, talk all la-di-da, worry her head reading a lot of heavy stuff, and wear herself out walking round art galleries? It's all a lot of nonsense, in my opinion. Our Rose should have stuck to Len Hobbs. Look at him now, there's a go-ahead for you. After the mill shut down, Len got a job in a garage and now he's in the way of starting up on his own. He thought the world of our Rose, he did.'

By this time Rose was having a little weep and complaining yet again about her husband, his work and their social life. She was utterly bored living in the country, seeing only Gerald and his friends. And they could never keep servants because he'd never trust her relationship with them. As soon as she got friendly with them, Gerald became rude and overbearing, speaking to them as though they were the black servants he'd employed in Rhodesia, so naturally the servants gave in their notice. The only person who was nice to her was Mrs Wardham. Gerald was coming home late every night and Rose was sure that he was carrying on with another woman. As I'd heard this mournful saga many times, I interrupted the flow to say that I had to get back; adding, for Mrs Lawton's benefit, that since I had none of Rose's natural advantages, there was no danger of my making the transition – matrimonial wise – from below stairs to above. Her ma remarked somewhat caustically that if long words were a ladder, I'd be up above in no time at all.

I couldn't argue with Mrs Lawton, she was far too formidable; but I did not agree with her firmly held opinion that only disaster could follow a deviation from the master-servant relationship; that above and below stairs were so divided by class, education and lineage, they could never mix. If Rose had not been so stubborn and narrow-minded, so determined not to change from the Rose Lawton of a back street in Manchester to being Mrs Rose Wardham, mistress of a fine house and servants; if she had acknowledged her husbband's genuine desire to make his wife socially acceptable, then the marriage could have been a success.

But Rose was so dogmatic, stating that she wasn't going to be different from her parents and relations; for they'd say their Rose had gone all snooty. Gerald had fallen in love with her as a parlourmaid, why should he expect her to alter, to become what he called a lady. Before they were married, Gerald had said that he liked her Mancunian accent, it was so down to earth. Rose wasn't to bother her pretty head about books and things, he'd never liked brainy women.

In vain Mary and I pointed out that although no doubt Gerald had fallen in love with Rose's peach-like complexion, blue eyes and golden hair, these attributes alone were not enough for a lasting and successful marriage. She should tone down her voice, acquire just a veneer of polish, listen to and copy the social chit-chat of dinner party conversation. Armoured with this, and with her looks and the expensive clothes, she'd be the same as one of 'them'. She could always be just 'our Rose' when she was with us, or with her own family. It rankled with Rose that her husband's father would not acknowledge her as a daughter-in-law, would not even see Victoria Helen. But what did that matter? Gerald was independent financially, and his mother and sister were extremely kind to Rose.

I found myself thinking again how very little Rose contributed towards a happy marriage, especially in one of the most important aspects of it; sex, which she disliked, saying that it made her feel dirty. I imagined that her joyless, strict and church-going mother had never demonstrated physical affection either to her husband or child, and Rose was just the same. Though she never consciously tried to look seductive and desirable, she gave the impression of being very loving. But I was quite sure that any man who tried to get fresh with Rose would be rebuffed in no uncertain terms. It was easy for her to be a faithful wife because she never felt the slightest desire to stray. Once, when Rose was bitterly complaining to Mary and me that she was certain Gerald had another woman, I was irritated enough to say, 'What can you expect, when you have a separate bedroom and can't bear to have your husband in the same bed. What's he supposed to do, sit on ice?'

Rose was really upset by this, protesting that she did her duty, she never refused Gerald if he came into her room. Somehow, her saying that reminded me of the notice in the little grocer's shop at home; PLEASE DO NOT ASK FOR CREDIT, AS A REFUSAL OFTEN OFFENDS.

What a basis for a loving marriage, 'doing one's duty'! I was vain enough to feel that given the same chance as Rose, I'd have made a success of it.

Yet, talking about this in our servants' hall, nobody agreed with me. Mr Kite, steeped in the dignity of his position as a butler, was emphatic that no servant could ever be one of 'them above stairs', one had to be born into that class. I expected Mr Kite to hold such an opinion, but even Ada, Norma and Elsie thought that Rose had made the biggest mistake of her life in marrying one of the masters; Elsie ended the conversation by saying, 'They're them, and we're us, and I wouldn't want to change that'.

In any case, unfortunately for me, it seemed as though I'd never have the opportunity to make a success of any kind of marriage. The absence of any young man prepared to take me on for life was enough to make me despair of ever leaving domestic service. Mary and I agreed that a pretty face was *the* attribute needed to attract a man, few men having enough sense to realise that a pretty face alone wouldn't cook for them or darn their socks. When I thought of all the 'possibles' that I'd fed with titbits in my kitchen, only to discover that most of them already had girlfriends, I almost gave up the pursuit of matrimony. Mary was even more despondent than I was. Months ago, when she'd heard from her merchant navy boyfriend that he'd married a girl in Australia – evidently the understanding between him and Mary hadn't been understood by *him* – Mary had determined to marry the first man who asked her; the first man had been Alfred. When that engagement was broken off, poor Mary lost confidence for a while in her ability to attract the opposite sex. Then, when she saw the young and handsome butler in her new place, her hopes rose again, but not for long. She found that the young and handsome butler had an antipathy to females, he much preferred the younger, even more handsome valet. I nobly refrained from saying 'I told you so'.

Marriage seemed to be in the air at this time, judging by the people we knew who were about to take on a man for better or for worse. But perhaps Mary and I were not breathing the right air.

25

O dette was all set to marry Armand, the son of the man who owned the local estaminet. She told us, with typical French shrewdness, that her beau-père to be was very old, it wouldn't be long before she and Armand were running the estaminet. Two weeks before Odette left England, her cousin Annette arrived to take Odette's place as a lady's maid. Much to the relief of Mr Kite, whose idea of French girls was that they were all pert, given to making saucy remarks and with no respect for their elders – like Odette in fact – her cousin Annette was a timid and mousey girl. Even if she hadn't been, her knowledge of the English language was limited to some dozen words, so as she gazed respectfully at our butler she probably thought his ponderous remarks were words of wisdom.

Our butler had been fed up to the teeth to hear Elsie and Odette talking about their future husbands; and now, to make matters worse, Mrs Van Lievden had her niece staying in the house who, according to Mr Kite, had only come here from Holland to secure an English husband. Madam was going to launch her into English society, and all the talk in the dining-room was about jewels, dresses and dances. When asked what was wrong in Madam's niece wanting to marry an Englishman, Mr Kite said he didn't hold with foreigners. To hear our butler say 'foreigners', one would have thought Miss Van Lievden was a Hottentot.

Madam gave Elsie a beautiful clock as a wedding present, and we all clubbed together to buy her a case of knives. Elsie wanted me to be one of her bridesmaids but, remembering the old saying 'three times a bridesmaid never a bride', I refused the honour. I'd been a bridesmaid twice as a child, and although I didn't really believe in such superstitions, nevertheless, on such an important issue, I didn't dare to tempt fate. Norma, Ada and I were given an extra day off to go to the wedding; in fact, Madam was kind enough to let us travel down to Kent on the previous evening so that we could have the whole day there. The other servants; Mr Kite, the new head housemaid, Constance, and the kitchenmaid would have an extra day later on. Elsie's mother put us up for the night in her cottage; we all slept in one huge bed with a feather mattress. None of us wanted to be the one in the middle so we tossed for it, Ada lost. The cottage was very pretty, creeper-covered and thatched roof, just like a picture-postcard cottage. But of course postcards cannot show the drawbacks to what appears to be picturesque – and here they couldn't have shown the tiny leaded window panes that excluded the sunlight, the lack of piped-water, electricity and drainage, the erratic path – well, erratic anyway in the pitch dark for visitors – to the primitive lavatory at the bottom of the garden. To us three city girls, one night only was a laughable experience, but I'm sure we'd never have coped with the lack of amenities as did Elsie's mum. She'd always lived in the cottage and was used to it.

The small village church was almost full with Elsie and Jack's relations. Both families must have been prolific breeders, but not difficult I suppose considering how early one goes to bed in the country. Elsie looked really lovely in her white dress. I was pleased to be there, and I was also envious of her good fortune, being unaware then that not so many months would elapse before I too would become legally tied to a man – though not in a church. At the reception, judging by the fond looks and kisses Elsie was giving Jack, she'd forgotten about her desire to be independent.

I suppose the wedding was like all such occasions. Telegrams were read out, such as 'May all your troubles be little ones'; the usual witticisms were passed, and one was that Elsie could never be accused of 'marrying in haste to repent at leisure'. The best man kissed the bridesmaid; we three girls, under the influence of strong cider, kissed any man who showed the slightest disposition to kiss us – and even, I'm afraid some who didn't. In the square dance I had as my partner a brawny, beefy bull-necked man, who every time he whirled me round – and off my feet – shouted, 'Up girl, up girl'. When the dance was over, I felt as though I'd been put through a mangle. Norma just laughed saying, 'Well, you got a man, any port in a storm!' But I didn't feel that my position was as stormy as all that.

We waved Elsie and Jack off to their honeymoon in Bournemouth, the bride's mother wept as every mother seems to do when her daughter becomes a wife. Though, now I recollect it, my mother didn't weep when I got married. Perhaps Mum went along with 'Nothing is here for tears; nothing to wail or knock the breast'.

Our new head housemaid, Connie as she liked to be called, was long past the age of matrimony, being about fifty-five years old. She was forty-five before she went into domestic service, having then, as she put it, 'fallen on hard times'. The youngest of five children, it was Connie's lot in life to look after her aged parents with no help from the other four. The one and only possible husband had rapidly cooled off when he discovered that marrying Connie meant having her aged parents to live with them. Her mother died at seventy-five, followed five years later by her exceedingly cantankerous father. When he died, his civil service pension ended. Without a trace of self-pity in her voice, Connie said to us:

'There was I, fair, fat and nearly forty-five, with no money, a rented house and no assets save the furniture. My married brothers and sisters descended on the home like vultures, saying that as they had children they needed extra things, that mother had promised them this and that; regardless of the fact that it was I who'd looked after the home all through the years. Oh! they offered me a home with them, but I found I was an unpaid drudge and baby-minder. Suddenly, I said to myself, don't be a stupid woman, for years you've done housework for nothing but pocket-money, why not go into service, get your board and lodge and earn a wage as well? So, with a good reference from the vicar, I got a lovely job. Stayed there ten years until my Madam died. Now I'm here.'

'Did she leave you anything in her will?' asked Ada.

'Yes, dear, she left me a brooch and three months' wages. Not enough to retire on as the brooch is only worth £50. But I don't want to retire, I like being in serivice. This Madam isn't quite as nice as my old Madam, she took a personal interest in us, but it's very comfortable here. I shall stay as long as possible.'

Mr Kite fully approved of such sentiments, as he too intended to be a butler as long as his age and health allowed.

Now that Mrs Van Lievden had her eighteen-year-old niece staying in the house, a lot more entertaining was done. I quite enjoyed the extra cooking and trying out new recipes. It's very pleasant being a cook when one doesn't have housework and shopping to do as well. I could telephone the tradesmen for all I needed, and I had a kitchenmaid to clean, wash-up and do all the vegetables. Bessie's successor was named Miriam, she said all her family had biblical names; her brothers were Joshua and Samuel, her sisters Ruth and Abigail. I asked Miriam if her mother was always reading the Bible, and Miriam laughed at this, saying. 'Poor Mum's never had time to read anything. She's had to work to keep us. My dad drank like a fish, spent all his wages on the stuff whenever he was in work – which wasn't often. When he was drunk, he knocked Mum about and us kids too. One night, as drunk as a lord, he fell in the Thames and got drowned; Mum wept a bit but none of us kids did.'

I thought perhaps Miriam's mother gave all her children biblical names as an oblation to the Lord, hoping he would provide as it was certain her husband wouldn't.

For a fifteen-year-old, Miriam was far more sophisticated and confident than I had been when I started as a kitchenmaid, and she wasn't in the least in awe of the butler. In fact, far from protecting her from Mr Kite's reprimands, as Mrs Buller had protected me from Mr Hall's sarcastic wit, I sometimes had to tell Miriam, in private, that she really mustn't argue and disagree so often with Mr Kite. It made for discord in the servants hall.

'Cook, I'll willingly do anything you ask me to do in the way of work, because that's my job. But my mum was in service and she warned me about butlers, said that some of them, especially if they were old family retainers, thought they were God Almighty below stairs and that they ran the staff. Mum said butlers can't tell housemaids and the kitchen staff what to do, only their footmen and parlourmaids. So I'm not having Mr Kite coming the great "I am". You don't do it, Cook.'

Such opinions from a lowly kitchenmaid were calculated to upset the rigid hierarchy of servants below stairs. I sharply told Miriam that all under servants were expected to keep quiet in the servants' hall; that because the upper servants monopolised the conversation, they weren't 'putting on' the under servants.

But Miriam was far more helpful to me than Bessie had been. She was quick, willing and eager to learn how to cook vegetables and make sauces. Her one drawback was a tendency to laugh immoderately at anything remotely resembling a joke. Strangely, Connie became very fond of Miriam and was almost like a mother to her. Perhaps it was the attraction of opposites. Connie had had too much home life and Miriam far too little. Miriam, in her first place of domestic service, was surprised at our standard of comfort. She'd heard from her mother that in the servants' sparse leisure time, they sat in a dark and dingy servants' hall and slept in freezing cold or sweltering hot attic bedrooms; nothing whatever was done to make servants comfortable. I warned Miriam that not all situations were as good as this one; that when I'd worked for a Mrs Hunter-Jones, we hadn't even a servants' hall, we sat on hard chairs in a miserable kitchen, used chipped crockery and our bedroom was just as spartan. Miriam reckoned she could stay in a place like this for ever, she'd never get married and have a life like her mum's. I had no desire to stay in the place for ever, probably Miriam would change her opinion when she'd had ten years of being below stairs. Gladys had once irreverently compared our life to being in a nunnery, with a few castrated monks to add to our frustrations. Mary and I had protested it wasn't as bad as that; look what happened to Rose, we'd added.

Both Mary and I had had a letter from Rose, asking us to come and see her again as soon as we had a whole day free. So we wrote and carefully arranged a day this time; Mary remarked caustically that she didn't want a repetition of our first visit.

26

This time, having no kind Mr Davies to drive us, we had to make the journey by train. I was amused to discover that Mary had brought an ample supply of sandwiches and bars of chocolate, as though we were setting out on a hazardous mission where no sustenance would be provided. But it was only too true, as Mary pointed out, that on none of the occasions we'd visited Rose in Hampstead, had we ever sat down to a banquet. Not that we arrived at our destination well-laden with supplies, because in our compartment were two young men – Mary having walked the length of the train in an endeavour to find what she called, 'somebody lively' for us to talk to. For sure Sid and Joe were lively enough, if a disclosure of all the pictures they'd seen, dances they'd been to and the girls they'd known constituted liveliness, but I disliked both of them, especially the one who kept saying apropos of some girl he'd taken home from a dance, 'Cor, she wasn't 'alf a bit of orl right'. Conversation aside, they certainly had voracious appetites, consuming Mary's sandwiches as though their next meal wouldn't be until sometime in the dim and distant future. When we were in the bus on our way to Rose's home, I mocked Sid and Joe's appalling English: 'This bus ain't 'alf slow', I said. Mary accused me of being a snob, which perhaps I was; but although being in domestic service didn't give one a public school accent, it did teach one to speak correctly. Which was why I got so annoyed when servants were portrayed on the stage as figures of fun dropping their aitches even oftener than the male lead dropped his trousers.

Mary and I were extremely surprised, and certainly not very pleased, to find that Rose's mother and aunt were also in the house, having arrived an hour earlier. We recollected the occasion when we had called on Mrs Lawton in Kensington one afternoon, to see she had everything she needed. Our reception was not such as to encourage us to repeat the occasion. She did make us a cup of tea, yes. But then we sat on the edge of the green plush chairs, sipping the hot and over-sweet stuff, while she told us that Mr. Lawton was out searching for work, that she disliked people arriving without warning, and that she was sure she'd never like London or Londoners, they seemed an ungodly lot; the only decent person she'd met was the curate from the Presbyterian church. In view of all the time we'd given up, and the work we'd done to make her rooms comfortable, I thought Mary and I were justified in feeling annoyed by such a lukewarm welcome.

So now, while we were in the bathroom tidying-up, I said to Mary that we were not to let ourselves be intimidated by Rose's mother, we weren't unexpected visitors, we'd been invited. Though, I whispered, 'I don't know why we're here. Rose looks much as usual, no great calamity seems to have happened. I don't know about you, Mary, but I wouldn't have come if I'd known those two would be here. Well, I don't mind the aunt, but her ma gives me the creeps. All she talks about is sinners and righteousness and nobody is perfect in the sight of the Lord; if that's what religion does for you, I'll stay an agnostic.'

We found them sitting round the table in Rose's own small sitting-room as though they were waiting for a seance to begin. Uncle Fred's wife, Amelia Green, although better-dressed than when we had last seen her, still looked lack-lustre and timid, especially in comparison with Mrs Lawton. And Mrs Lawton was saying, in an angry voice, that Rose never brought Victoria Helen to see her; and that even now she couldn't see her only grandchild because Rose had sent her away.

'I didn't send her away,' protested Rose, 'her Aunt Helen fetched her over a week ago. She loves having Victoria to stay with her and I get such headaches having the child around, she's so noisy.'

Gerald's sister, Helen, had inherited enough money from an old great-aunt to enable her to become independent of her father, Mr Wardham. She'd promptly left Redlands and was now living in the country with a woman friend. Nowadays, two women living together for economy and companionship risk being labelled as lesbians but, from the little I knew of Miss Helen I'm sure it was a perfectly innocent relationship; her friend was a painter and Miss Helen was trying to write. According to Rose, Mr Wardham was furious that his daughter had left home; now he'd only got his wife to bully. He'd ranted at her, saying a fine couple of children *she'd* brought up; her son married to a slut and her daughter, no man being a fool enough to marry her, had got a woman instead. I thought, that's just like a man. If his family follow what he considers the right pattern in life, then he will proudly boast of 'my son, my daughter', But if they rebel, then his wife learns that the children are hers.

When Rose told us we were having an early lunch, I had difficulty in suppressing a laugh as I thought of Mary's parcel of sandwiches. How fortunate they'd been eaten on the train.

Rose's mother snapped 'Lunch, what d'you mean, lunch? You were brought up to call the midday meal, dinner. It's always dinner to your father and me.'

To Mary and me that lunch – or dinner – was an hilarious experience; we'd have liked to have heard what Rose's cook and parlourmaid were saying in the kitchen. It was easy to see that Mrs Lawton and Aunt Amelia felt extremely uncomfortable being waited on by a servant, and the meal was enlivened by both of them bobbing up and down collecting the plates, serving the vegetables and generally taking over the duties of Maud, the house-parlourmaid. If only I could have photographed the expression on Maud's face as she surveyed this new kind of guest. Mary and I still had no idea why we'd been invited and, from the way her mother avoided speaking to us, we could sense that she found our presence unwelcome. I heard her mutter to Rose that it was a family matter and outsiders, meaning Mary and me, shouldn't be brought into it. Rose said we weren't outsiders; we were her best and only friends. And she added sharply, that we'd run all over London looking for a decent place for her parents to live in.

During the meal, Aunt Amelia complained that Fred didn't like his job as a lift man; going up and down all day made him feel giddy when he got home. Mary put her foot in it by saying surely he was used to going up and down in a coal mine.

'That shows you Southerners know nothing about the North,' snapped Mrs. Lawton, 'Men are not constantly going up and down in a coal mine. They go down and stay down until their shift is over. Anyway,' she added, to Aunt Amelia, 'your Fred's got a better job than my Joe's in the factory. He's doing the same thing all day over and over again and there's no skill in the work like there was in the mill.'

Considering her Joe's weeks of unemployent in Manchester and the fact that he had found work within two weeks of being in London, I reckon he'd no cause to complain.

Mrs Lawton refused to drink coffee after the meal, saying she didn't hold with such outlandish notions; a cup of good strong tea was what she wanted. We retired to the sitting-room, sat round the table again and Rose told us, quite calmly, without any tears or histrionics, that Gerald wanted a divorce. If she had said that her husband wanted to murder her, the news couldn't have been more calamitous as far as her mother was concerned. For a few minutes that formidable woman was speechless. Then, not bothering to ask Rose any questions, she burst out:

'Divorce? Never! Whoever heard of such a thing! The *disgrace* of it. I'd never dare show my face in the old street. There's never been such a thing in our family, we've always been respectable hard-working people. What will the Reverend think when he knows?

You was married all proper, Rose, and "those whom God had joined together, let no man put asunder".'

'It's a woman who wants to put it asunder, Ma, as well as a man.'

'That I should live to hear my daughter, who was brought up in as God-fearing a home as any in the street, talk about marriage in that light way. And what about Victoria Helen, what's going to happen to her? Marriage is for life, through good times and bad, it can't be broken just because one of the partner's wants to break it. Young people today have no morals, marriage means nothing sacred to them,' and she looked at Mary and me with accusing eyes, as though it was our fault. I resented this silent accusation, especially so as we were two single girls trying our hardest to enter into the matrimonial state. Our first question to Rose was, why did her husband want a divorce, did he want to marry some other woman?

'Yes, he does,' said Rose, bitterly, 'And you'd never guess who he's fallen for. To think that I welcomed her here so many times and she made out to be my friend, helping me with the guests and all. Yet all the time her and Gerald were carrying on behind my back. But she'll never be able to marry my husband because I won't give him a divorce. Why should I? I've done nothing wrong, not even so much as kissed another man since I married.'

'Who is she, Rose, who is she?' we asked impatiently.

'She's Sheila Frost, the wife of Gerald's partner Ron. That's who she is. I never liked Ron, he was always making stupid jokes, and if he was anything of a man he'd punch Gerald on the nose. But they're not even breaking the partnership, they're both away up North on a business trip. If you ask me, Ron's glad to be rid of his wife.'

'My advice to you, Rose,' said her ma, not waiting to be asked to give her opinion, 'is to ignore the whole thing; it will blow over. Men always have been stupid creatures who don't know their own minds. In six months' time, your Gerald will have got tired of that woman.'

'I don't care whether he has or not, Ma, I'm going to get a legal separation. I'm going back to London. I'll get a nice little house where me and Vicky can live; Gerald will have to support us.'

Roses's voice changed from its unaccustomed calmness to shrill denunciation, she said she was sick to death of her husband trying to make her into a lady. She never again wanted to hear that her accent was an assault on his ears; that her ignorance of what went on in the world regarding politics, music and the arts, could only be equalled by a native of darkest Africa. She was fed up living in the country, where county people looked down on her and, although the village people were ever so nice, she could never invite them to the house. She, Rose, never had, and never would get used to servants waiting on her. In her own little house, she could look after herself and Vicky and have peace and quiet. She and Gerald had endless quarrels, and when he'd had too much to drink which happened often, he'd taunt her by saying that he could have made a better wife out of the black girl who worked for him in Rhodesia.

'He probably seduced her too,' Rose added rancorously.

Here her mother interrupted to say, sharply, 'What d'you mean, "seduced her too"? He never took advantage of you, you was married all right and proper, your pa saw to that. I warned you, you should have stuck to Len.'

'Perhaps Rose didn't love Len,' interposed Aunt Amelia, in a deprecating voice.

'You be quiet, Melia. What's love got to do with it? That's not what marriage is all about. Marriage is leaving your parents' home to look after your man, have his kids, make one shilling go as far as five, and keep a clean, respectable and God-fearing home.'

Mary and I looked at each other and I knew the same thought was in her mind; that such a description of marriage was far removed from our ideas on the subject.

In spite of another hour listening to her mother's admonitions on it being Rose's duty, if only for the sake of Victoria Helen, to remain with her husband – how could she if he wanted a divorce? – Rose was firm in her determination to seek a legal separation. When it was time to leave, we found to our consternation that Rose had ordered a car to take us to the station, we were all travelling on the same train. So much did Mrs Lawton overawe us that we hadn't the nerve to sit in a different compartment. The journey back to London was certainly different from our journey down when Mary had been looking for 'somebody lively'. Neither Rose's ma nor Aunt Amelia even remotely resembled lively people. In fact, judging by Mrs Lawton's dour expression and few grudging remarks, she held us personally responsible for her daughter's misfortune.

Back at our local, our spirits lightened considerably over a glass of port and lemon, and a few jokes with Morgan the barman. After a second glass, Mary, giggling, said, 'If that old dragon of a woman could see us now, she'd be on her knees praying for our souls – what time she wasn't upbraiding her daughter for having such immoral friends. Margaret, did you notice what Rose said about the black girl, "seduced her too". D'you think Rose slept with Gerald before they were married'?

'I wouldn't think so, Mary. Rose would have thought it a mortal sin. In fact, I belive that Rose thinks having relations with one's husband is mortal sin, unless it's for the purpose of having children. And I hope Rose doesn't expect us to find her a house in London, we've done our duty looking for her ma's place.'

'I wonder if Morgan's married' said Mary. I could tell that all this talk about the matrimonial state had forcibly reminded her of her single status.

'Of course he is, Mary. Why he's fifty if he's a day. But you wouldn't want to marry a barman, look at the awkward hours they work.'

'I'd marry the devil himself to get out of domestic service, I've had too much of it,' said Mary. She had had three glasses of port and lemon by this time and had become quite lachrymose. Fortunately it was time to leave so, both of us sucking our Phul-Nana cachous – I didn't want staid Mr Kite to know I'd been drinking – we went back to our respective basements.

27

On our one free day each month we were allowed occasionally as a rare treat to stay out until midnight. If we went to a dance this was a great advantage as far as getting an escort home was concerned. Although we were constantly hearing that we'd never find a decent young man at a dance, it was certain that at least we would find a few unattached males there. The young ladies above stairs could meet young men in what I called the proper way, by being introduced to them at debs' coming-out parties and other social occasions, but where could servant girls meet the opposite sex? There were no clubs for us, for one thing our hours were too erratic. So we picked them up wherever we could; at a dance, in Hyde Park or a Lyons teashop.

Realising that I'd been on what then seemed a fairly long train journey, Mr Kite was agreeably surprised to see me back at eleven o'clock; he'd never go to bed until he'd made sure that every door was bolted. It was not necessary, nor was it part of his duties in the place to wait up for me; I had a key to the basement door and was capable of seeing that all was safe before I retired. But our butler was loth to relinquish a task which, in his previous situations, had always been his prerogative. I'm sure that he saw himself as the strong male servant guarding the lives – and morals – of the flighty maids. Furthermore, Mr Kite never forgot that his grandfather had held the very highest position open to domestic servants; he was steward in a stately country house. It had to be an extremely wealthy family that employed a steward, because such a high position meant that he had a retinue of house servants under him. In such large establishments, where the ordinary servants seldom saw their employers, the steward and the housekeeper were the bosses.

Perhaps I flattered myself, but I thought Mr Kite rather liked the rare occasions when he and I sat up over a cup of cocoa when the others had gone to bed, talking about previous situations and employers. Domestic service was, and would always be, Mr Kite's whole life – I hoped that it wouldn't be mine. But although he had worked below stairs for many more years than I had, I did know about those even harder times through my mother, who started in service as a between-maid – the worst job of the lot. So now as we sat down at the kitchen table to drink our cocoa, with me hoping that an aura of Phul-Nana cachous was being wafted towards Mr Kite – and not port and lemon – he began to reminisce of the days when he worked in real stately homes, such as the house where Mr Penny had been the imposing butler.

'You'd not have found him such a lively man in those days, Cook,' and I sensed that our obvious enjoyment of Mr Penny's tales had rankled with the butler.

'Mind you,' added Mr Kite magnanimously, 'he couldn't afford to be too carefree, he'd have lost his authority over us menservants; as it was, James, the second footman, Sam the pageboy and I went in mortal dread of Horace Penny. He never told you his name was Horace, did he? Behind his back we used to call him "horrid penny". It's true he was a good-looking man and, in spite of what he told you about that Jezebel, he was a great one for the girls. Mrs Allen, the cook, would never leave her kitchen girls alone with our butler, not even in the daytime. Although it was all kept quiet, we servants knew that he seduced and got into the family way, Cissie, the head gardener's daughter – and her, with a bit of education and all. Horace Penny was scared stiff that he'd have to marry Cissie, that would have cooked his goose with the village girls. Lucky for him, George, our second gardener, was in love with the girl and married her. 'But,' and Mr Kite smiled at the memory, 'he made Horace Penny fork out £50 of his savings to buy their furniture. Horace Penny couldn't bear the idea of being tied down. Ah! Those were the days of *real* domestic service. Huge staff, houses full of guests, parties and balls; we servants lived like fighting-cocks. This place can't be compared with the old days.'

'Did you never want to get married, Mr Kite?'

'Never, Cook. Don't get me wrong, I admire and respect the ladies, but I've never loved but one lady in my life, and that was my mother. I'm not saying I didn't have my chances of holy matrimony – I took that statement with a pinch of salt; nobody likes to admit that there was never a single person who wanted to take them on for life – 'but Mother and I were so close, I never met a woman who could compare with her. I did once take a young lady to see Mother – she was the housemaid's sister – but afterwards Mother said to me "My son, you have nothing to do with that young woman. She'll come to no good, you mark my words." Mother was right, as usual, for the girl gave up being a parlourmaid; said she was sick of working a sixteen-hour day with no handle to her name and a bloody white blob on her head. Excuse the language, Cook, but that's the sort of person she turned out to be and' – here Mr Kite lowered his voice to a sepulchral utterance – 'she finished up on the streets.'

As I realised Mr Kite would be unable to see that I was getting at him, I said, sententiously, 'Perhaps if you had married her, Mr Kite, she might have been a good woman.'

'That's true, Cook. But it would have upset Mother. Mother was such a wonderful person, always worrying about whether I was well and happy.'

Unwilling to listen to further panegyrics about his mother, I gave a yawn and said it was time that I went to bed, tomorrow would be a busy day. Mr Kite's conversation, never at any time calculated to raise one's blood pressure was, when one was tired, a positive soporific. But for all his prosiness and narrow outlook, he was a kind-hearted man; for when I'd spoken about Uncle Fred's wife being so poor, Mr Kite had given me money for the children and insisted that I was not to mention the money was given by him.

Our busy tomorrow was because Mrs Van Lievden's niece, Elsa, was having an engagement dinner at our house. Though her intended was an Englishman, she'd originally met him in Amsterdam – something to do with the buying and selling of diamonds. Our chauffeur, Ewan Davies, remarked sourly that no doubt the niece, failing to find a possible husband among her own countrymen, had chased Mr Harrison from Amsterdam to London. Before the arrival of the niece, Mr Davies had been used to a fair amount of free time, now he found himself driving Madam and the niece to the shops and hairdresser every morning, and to some function or other every evening. So, as was only natural, our normally good-tempered chauffeur felt 'put-upon', forgot all the months of easy-living and thought only that he was working long hours for an outsider. When I pointed out that it was just the same for all of us servants, he disagreed.

'It's not the same at all, Cook. All of you sleep in, so you have to be here whether Madam entertains or not. But I don't consider myself a domestic servant, I'm used to being in my own home at a reasonable hour in the evening. The sooner that girl gets married the better, as far as I'm concerned, otherwise Madam can look for another chauffeur; with my reference I can soon get another job.'

Both he and I knew that was an empty threat; he'd be a long time finding as good a place as the Van Lievdens'.

There was a slight disagreement between Madam and me at this time. Because of the extra entertaining, at lunch and dinner parties, I'd really gone to town on the cooking and made several rather elaborate dishes. One morning, after Madam and I had worked out the menu, she got as far as the kitchen door and stopped.

'Oh, Cook, my niece was so impressed by the dinner last night, she would very much like to see you cooking. Would you mind if she came down one morning? Miss Elsa wouldn't interfere, just stand and watch you.'

Never in this world was my immediate thought. Not only did I recollect the previous time one of 'them' had invaded my domain, I genuinely disliked anybody – apart from my kitchenmaid – watching me cook. I can talk to people if they are sitting at one end of the kitchen, but to stand over me, never. Madam accepted this explanation, but I could tell from her slightly more austere manner subsequently, that she wasn't pleased. Not that I worried overmuch, my contact with Madam was only for half-an-hour in the morning and I knew she'd not want to lose a good cook. I didn't want to leave either, not unless I was leaving domestic service permanently, to get married. The others applauded my stand, none of them wanting a state of affairs where one of 'them' might suddenly come below stairs.

'It's a liberty, Cook, that's what it is,' complained Mr Kite. 'Why, none of us would dare to put our feet up in our own servants' hall for fear that the master or madam would be looking in on us. It's little privacy we have now with bells ringing all day long. I'm telling you, Cook, if the Master made a habit of coming into my pantry without warning, I'd soon give in my notice.'

Years of a life below stairs seemed to have given our butler the fixed idea that as accommodation was part of our wages, the basement was a sort of private flat for servants, no longer a part of the house. And it always annoyed me when our butler referred to Mr Van Lievden as 'the Master'. In vain did I point out that he wasn't our master, he was our employer. Just because we had to call them 'Sir and Madam', it didn't mean that they had powers of life and death over us.

Miriam put her oar in to say her mum had told her that most rich people who employed servants were nothing but parasites. Mr Kite was incensed to hear this.

'Nobody asked your opinion, Miss, you don't know anything about good service. Anyway, I don't suppose you know what a parasite is.'

But nobody could put down that Mariam as she answered, pertly, 'I do at that, it's fleas'.

Afterwards, I told her that she'd never survive in domestic service if she couldn't hold her tongue before the upper servants, it simply wasn't the done thing to contradict them. After all, it was the upper servants who had to listen to the complaints if anything went wrong; they got the blame from those above stairs, not the under servants.

Miriam got her militant ideas from her mother, who'd been brought up in an orphanage and gone into service at fourteen. Miriam's mother had told her that from the age of eleven, all the girls at the orphanage were unpaid laundry workers and cleaners; and when they left the orphanage to go into service – and that's where all of them went – they were treated harshly because the mistress knew they'd no real home. No wonder servants were ten-a-penny if all orphanages sent their girls there. But Miriam was a good worker and so grateful for anything I did for her. In my first place, as a kitchenmaid, Mrs McIlroy, the cook, had let me make a large fruit cake every week to take home to my parents – it hadn't occurred to me at the time that she was being generous with Madam's goods. Now I did the same for Miriam; our Madam could well afford a few extra raisins, eggs and sugar.

The engagement dinner was a great success, as were the three chauffeurs in our servants' hall, who looked very smart in their uniforms; green, brown and plum-coloured. Mr Penny came again and the washer-up for the kitchen. From the basement window I managed to get a glimpse of Miss Elsa's intended – mostly his legs, as he was about six feet tall. In my opinion, he wasn't exactly love's young dream, being about forty and already going bald. But perhaps Miss Elsa thought, better diamonds than a Don Juan.

It was a six-course dinner; for the entrée I made a salmi of duck and the main course was beef à la mode. During our supper, Mr Kite told me that he had heard the chief guest praising the entrée and the beef à la mode. 'Now's the time to ask Madam for a rise,' Mr Kite said, but of course no one would have ever dared to. Only when one left and applied for another place did one ask for a higher wage.

I'd noticed that the oldest of the chauffeurs, a Mr McGregor, was reading *Boswell's Life of Johnson*, so I sat him next to me at the supper table; it was not often I got the chance to talk about books. I told Mr McGregor that I'd picked up an 1874 edition of *Boswell's Life of Johnson*, for two shillings in the Portobello Road. I omitted to mention that I found the book heavy going and tedious, and, if Dr Johnson had said only half the things attributed to him by Boswell, it would still have been too much.

'Bought the book for two shillings, did you now,' said Mr McGregor. 'I borrowed my copy from the public library. Of course, I do indeed come from Scotland, but I cannot help it'.'

'That Sir, is what a very great many of your countrymen cannot help.'

We couldn't explain to the others what we were laughing about.

Our lady's maid, Annette, had by now been with us long enough to learn some English and Mick, the Irish chauffeur, was making her laugh by airing his knowledge of the French language – picked up when he was in France during the 1914–18 war. He sang, 'Mademoiselle from Armentières' but, as his version of the line 'Hasn't been kissed in forty years' was considerably different, reflecting as it did on Mademoiselle's constipation, our butler looked very disapproving. As so often when two or more servants were gathered together, the conversation eventually came around to talking about one's employers. On the assumption that derogatory remarks might have been heard upstairs, it was generally past employers who were discussed. I used to think that no other workers could find their employers such an absorbing topic of conversation as domestic servants found theirs. But then other workers could separate their work from their leisure; once they'd finished and were sitting in their own homes, it was a different life. Apart from one free day per month, one afternoon and evening and an alternate Sunday afternoon and evening, a servant's whole life was spent in the employer's home, it was therefore inevitable that the life of those upstairs should provide a diversion for us. So now John, the youngest, and the most handsome of the chauffeurs, was talking about his previous employer:

'The old man wasn't too bad, but the Madam was a holy terror, maids came and went like the wind in a colander. I was courting the parlourmaid, Gladys, and she told me that Madam was busy every morning making sure the maids had done their work properly. She'd rub her fingers along ledges, lift up the ornaments to see if they'd been dusted underneath, and she'd even deliberately drop money in obscure places not so much to make sure that the servants were honest, as to find out if they'd cleaned everywhere. All the servants were female – no man would have put up with her high and mighty manner. It didn't affect me so much because I didn't live in, I had a couple of rooms over the garage. The old man knew what she was like, and in an effort to keep servants he actually had a bathroom put in for them. Gladys said the way Madam carried on about providing this luxury for servants, you'd have thought she was giving them Buckingham Palace. The bathroom was on the floor below the attics where the servants slept and although there was a lavatory in it, Madam had forbidden the servants to use it during the night because she said the noise from the cistern woke her up. They had a cook at that time, old Mrs May, who was rather too fond of the gin bottle. One night, going down the stairs to the basement lavatory, carrying a lighted candle – every landing light was extinguished at night – Madam suddenly opened her bedroom door and called out, "Who's that, who's that?" Old Mrs May, half drunk, and irritable at having to go down to the basement, answered, "Well, it ain't bloody Santa Claus taken short, lucky for him in this place". Course, she got the sack next day but it was a laugh all right.'

We too laughed, and then Ada, the under-housemaid said, 'Oh, Mr Penny, do tell us one of your funny stories.'

Mr Penny, endeavouring to appear reluctant to take the limelight, and deprecating the idea that anybody wanted to listen to him, then said, 'You'd never believe this, though it's true as I'm sitting here at this table.'

'That's what you said the last time Mr Penny; of course we believe you.'

'Well, it happened when I was a young footman in a great house in Wiltshire. I went there in the beginning of December, I remember because the snow was thick on the ground. The old Master had just died at eighty years old, genuinely mourned by the servants. They all disliked his widow, thirty years younger and so mean that the butler said she'd have liked to have buried the coffin upright to save buying so much ground. She'd only married her husband for his money, and he was hardly cold in his grave, two months in fact, before she married an effeminate looking specimen of a man called Vivian – what a name for a man. When Christmas came, and they played at charades, he dressed up as a film vamp, makeup and all; and for sure looked the part.'

'Come on, Mr Penny, get to the exciting part, we can't sit here all night.'

'Well, I noticed that on Madam's bridge afternoons he always retired to his dressing-room and remained there for over two hours. One afternoon, being idle and full of curiosity, I peered through the keyhole – you'll never guess what I saw.'

'He had another woman there,' said Mick.

'He was drinking whisky' said Mr McGregor.

'No, nothing like that. There he was, dressed in the same women's clothes he'd worn for the charades, painted, powdered, lipsticked, a long golden wig on his head, sitting on a chair with one leg crossed over the other and' – here Mr Penny lowered his voice – 'I could see that he was wearing ladies' pink silk knickers. What do you think of that?'

'I think that it must have been an outsize keyhole for you to see all that,' said Mr Kite, sceptically.

Facetiously, Mick answered, 'Perhaps he was rehearsing for the next Christmas charades.'

'What! in January, it's not likely.'

We females were too taken aback to comment, or even to laugh. Bawdiness we could understand, but sexual aberration was outside our knowledge of life. In fact, we rather welcomed Connie commencing her usual paean of praise about her late employer, although we'd heard it many times. We all liked Connie, but she did get boring on the subject of her one and only domestic place. Because her Madam had no lady's maid, and was old and rather frail, she had depended on Connie for personal help.

'I used to go to church with her on Sundays and she'd often ask me to sit and read to her in the evening, or even just to be there for company. If any of her family came, I was just the same as them.'

That I didn't believe; a denizen of below stairs could never move up, unless, like Rose, she married into the social caste. Even if a servant could dress like them and use the correct speech, they would know she was a servant. We didn't have to be physically sub-servient, no curtseying or doffing of caps, but involuntarily there crept into one's voice a kind of subservience when talking to them above stairs.

So now, as I listened to Connie extolling the virtues of her late employer, I thought that I much preferred Mrs Van Lievden, who made no pretence of an interest in us personally but made sure that we had physical comforts.

Still, it was Connie who told Mary and me of a small house for sale in Streatham which she thought Rose would like and which, in fact, Rose's husband bought for her. Mary reckoned he was trying to sweeten Rose so that she would divorce him.

28

I'd never really believed that Rose would willingly give up her life at Greenlands. To leave all that wealth and comfort; a beautiful home, lovely gardens and servants to do the work, for a nondescript small house in Streatham; it seemed madness to me. But then I had never fully understood how much Rose hated the life, how alien she felt as the mistress of the establishment instead of the servant. Now that she was going to live in an ordinary house, Rose was a different person. She ceased to complain bitterly about her husband, his friends and way of life; although to Mary and me she attempted to justify her previous attitude.

'You see, when we fell in love, I'd no idea of living in a big house with servants, because I knew that Gerald had no money, apart from what Mrs Wardham gave him; I thought he'd get an ordinary job and we'd live in a small house like my ma's. After all,' Rose went on, somewhat plaintively, 'how could I know that he'd make a lot of money and want to live like a gentleman. When we married, he said that I was never to change, he loved me just as I was. And so he did, until he got rich and made all those society friends and those theatre people. Then I didn't fit in, I'd got to get educated and become a lady.'

Rose's idea that she and Victoria Helen would live harmoniously in a cosy little nest had a set-back as far as the child was concerned. She was a plain and unattractive child, already showing signs of her grandfather's ungovernable temper. Now she continually whined because she missed her huge nursery full of toys, her garden swing and see-saw; she probably missed her father too, he'd always made a fuss of her.

About two weeks after Rose had settled down in Streatham, Mary and I went over to see her on our free Sunday afternoon and evening – or rather Mary's free Sunday; as a cook I was free after lunch every Sunday. Mary looked resplendent in a new coat-frock of light brown gaberdine trimmed with dark brown braid. To be smartly and correctly dressed for the street, a costume or coat-frock was de rigueur at that time, the latter being cheapest to buy. No female ever went out hatless; Mary wore a brown cloche – or pudding basin hat – brown gloves and handbag. I'd saved my money to buy a bottle-green gaberdine costume with cloche to match, black patent shoes and black gloves. Gloves were another must, no matter how hot was the weather. We'd both used face powder, bought at Woolworths for sixpence a box. Perhaps ladies had their powder specially blended, but Woolworths had only three shades, white, pale pink and a kind of muddy-looking beige – we'd bought the pale pink. There was a subtle difference in using powder and lipstick; the former was acceptable but use of lipstick branded one as an 'easy catch', so we used white lip-salve – at least it made our lips shine. We generally used 'ashes of violet' perfume – also bought at Woolworths. Mary and I thought we looked like a couple of fashion-plates as we walked through Hyde Park; we certainly got a few wolf whistles. Mary was happy because for some time now she'd had a new boyfriend, a pal of the faithless Sid. I'd remonstrated, saying that after her experience with Sid, surely she could see there was no point in having a boyfriend who went on long voyages. Absence didn't make the heart grow fonder, it merely made it accustomed to absence.

'It's different this time, Margaret. I've been to his home, his parents were very nice to me. Conrad's not going to stay an AB, he's going to work his way up, his father was a chief engineer on a ship.

Besides, Conrad does short trips, he's away only three months. His dad's quite an educated man, he's got a whole shelf of books by authors like Melville and Joseph Conrad. He told me he reads them over and over again; that's why he called his son Conrad. I think it's a much nicer name than Sid.'

Well, Mary was right about the name. Nevertheless, I wouldn't have felt secure in the affections of a young man I saw only at three-monthly intervals.

On the journey to Streatham, I remarked to Mary that surely Rose would agree to a divorce for, even after it was granted, Gerald would still have to wait some time before he could marry again. Besides, what was the point of being legally tied to a man who no longer cared about you. He would support Rose until she married again, and she'd certainly have the opportunity for she was still very pretty.

'I could take a bet with you, Margaret, that Rose will never agree to a divorce. I've known her longer than you have and, although she seems to be soft and non-argumentative, she can be as hard as nails if she thinks she's right. Just think how she refused all Gerald's attempts to make her an 'above stairs' person. Besides, although Rose would be the innocent party in a divorce, she'd still look on it as a disgrace. No, Rose will never give him a divorce, of that I'm sure. And I'm equally sure she'll never want to marry again, if only because she dislikes the bed part.'

'Perhaps we'll be the same when we get married, Mary; not like the bed part, I mean. One never knows in advance, does one?'

'I don't see why we shouldn't like it, Margaret. Aunt Ellie did and I reckon it helped to finish off old Mack. She was always complaining to me about what she called, his "weasel", saying she had to spend a long time making it bark and even then its bite wasn't very powerful. Have you ever seen one, Margaret?'

'Well, I've seen what passed for one on statues and I had that glimpse when I went into Mrs Bishop's bathroom. But if you mean, have I given the object a detailed study, the answer is No; time and circumstances not allowing.'

'Oh, Margaret, you're awful,' and we laughed so loudly that the bus conductor came upstairs to share the joke. We told him that we were discussing anatomy. He knew what the word meant because he said he preferred to study astronomy, there were fewer complications.

The outside of the very ordinary semi-detached house in Streatham gave no indication of the almost opulent-furnished interior. Most of the furnishings had come from Greenlands, including as much of Rose's elaborate bedroom suite as her smaller room could take. I was amused to see that her favourite love-story magazines were no longer in a neat pile on the bedside table, but scattered over the bed now that she was free of the necessity to conceal them. All of the six rooms were overcrowded with furniture and ornaments. It seemed as though Rose had claimed ownership to as much as possible, perhaps as an insurance against future hard times. She'd already got friendly with her neighbour and had invited her in to have a cup of tea with us. Mrs Richard was a bright, bird-like kind of person, and she twittered like one too. I could tell that she was astonished to see such obviously expensive furnishings, and her eyes were busy making an inventory of Rose's possessions. We had tea in what Rose, with no pretensions at all, called the front room; Mrs Richard called it the drawing-room. Now that there were no servants to cut dainty, minute cucumber or egg sandwiches, or produce a plate of little fairy cakes, Rose had provided a far more substantial meal. There were corned-beef and tinned salmon sandwiches, doughnuts, lemon-cheese tarts and heavy plum cake. The cakes came from the bakers' shop as Rose hadn't yet learned much in the way of cooking. Mrs Richard kept up a non-stop flow of twittering:

'I said to Mr Richard when he came back – Mr Richard's away a lot – there's such a nice-looking person moved in next door, with a sweetly pretty little girl.'

Mary and I didn't dare look at each other; nobody in their right mind could call Victoria Helen 'sweetly pretty'.

The neighbour twittered on, 'I said to Mr Richard, "well, now our new neighbour really looks a lady"' – I saw Rose wince at this – '"maybe she'll be company for me you being away such a lot". I don't mind telling you, just between the four of us, that this road's not what it was when we first moved in. There used to be a nice class of people here, cleaned their windows, spotless white curtains, polished brass on the front door and every Sunday they'd be tidying the front garden. You'd never believe it to look at these houses, but some of the people haven't a penny to their name, they shouldn't be living in this kind of neighbourhood. I wouldn't mix with them even though I'm alone so much; Mr Richard has to go away you know.'

She must have told us half-a-dozen times that Mr Richard had to go away, but never once did she explain where, and why he went. We'd nearly finished tea when who should arrive, unexpected and unwelcome, but Rose's parents. Well, perhaps not so unwelcome this time as their arrival did get rid of Mrs Richard. One look at the formidable Mrs Lawton, and a far fiercer bird than a twittering sparrow would have been vanquished.

Mary and I, having spent nearly all our money on new finery, and our monthly wages not due for another week, we were prepared to stay with Rose for the afternoon and evening; no amount of hostility, suppressed or overt, would make us depart before time. Even Rose had admitted that her mother was a domineering and ill-natured woman, yet Mrs Lawton had always tried to give the impression that it was *Mr* Lawton who was the dogmatic one.

Before Rose left home to go into domestic service she was continually hearing, 'your father flatly forbids you to go to a dance, join a club, come home late from the pictures' – in reality it was her mother who put a ban on any form of enjoyment. Similarly, when her mother was talking to Aunt Amelia, it was always, 'Joe won't have it, Joe put his foot down'. In actual fact, though far from effusive in his welcome to us, saying nothing but 'How do', Mr Lawton didn't mind us being there. It was only when he talked of the 'bosses' that he became eloquent with bitter denunciations of what he called 'the system'.

Although Gerald's charm had worked on Mr Lawton enough to

get a grudging consent to the marriage, he'd very soon gone back to his original opinion of the 'bosses'. I'd have expected him to feel gratified in seeing, in the failure of his daughter's marriage, how right he'd been in asserting that there never could be an alliance between the upper class and working class, but I think that while saying 'I told you so', he was secretly irritated because Rose hadn't made a go of it.

Rose offered to make some fresh tea but Mrs Lawton said it was a waste; she should put boiling water on what was left in the pot. This at any rate indicated to Mary and me that she wasn't going to sponge on her daughter. I didn't know what financial arrangements had been made for Rose, but there was no shortage of food and comforts. We attempted to make light conversation, excluding such topics as work, marriage and the pleasures of living in London, knowing that a mention of any of these three acted as a touch-paper to her parents.

Rose said, brightly, 'I've had a letter from Aunt Amelia. She wrote that they have had a bit of luck, Uncle Fred has had a rise.'

Mary, with misplaced humour in view of Mrs Lawton's grim expression, said, 'That can't be much of a change surely? In his job he's getting a rise all day long.'

Our laughter quickly faded when Mr Lawton said angrily that he was sick of his job in the factory making electrical components; it was monotonous and, unless one worked overtime, ill paid too.

'There's no skill to it,' he complained, 'anybody could do the job. I'm a nothing there, a nobody. At the mill I was looked up to, I knew my job, and the men respected me.'

'Couldn't you look for a better job, Da?' asked Rose, timidly.

'What better job, where would I get it? All I was offered was the factory job or to be a lavatory attendant. Did you ever hear the like? That the day would come when I'd be offered a job cleaning out a men's lavatory – I'd sooner starve. And now we're going to have a national government; what good will that do? It's the same old lot that got the country into this mess. The only man who's got any sense in that lot is Maxton.'

After listening to many more fulminations, I began to feel that as a way of spending a pleasant Sunday afternoon, it left much to be desired. Born into a later generation, Mr Lawton would, without a doubt, have been a militant striker on the picket line, angrily insisting on workers' rights.

Yet there was one vast difference between the terrible Depression of the early thirties and living in England now. In spite of Mr Lawton's bitterness against the government, he, and the tens of thousands like him who'd lost their jobs and were living on the poverty line, never resorted to the violence and vandalism that prevails today. Nobody of my generation could ever have dreamed that the day would come in England when it wasn't safe to walk through the streets in the evening for fear of being mugged, when quiet country lanes and city parks were to be avoided if one was alone. How smugly did we read about the violence in America and say, 'It can't happen here'. Of course there always have been people who are just plain 'bad', but at one time if they were caught, they had to pay for their crimes; now they get therapy.

By the time Rose's father had finished his imprecations against the government, with special execrations for Ramsay MacDonald and Philip Snowden – he considered them responsible for the Labour landslide – he was too exhausted for general conversation. But his wife nobly kept things going by talking about the difference between north country people and Londoners – to the disparagement of the latter. If they'd had a sense of humour I'd have hummed:

'It's the same the whole world over,
It's the poor wot gets the blame;
It's the rich wot gets the pleasure,
Ain't it all a blooming shame'.

But faced with Mr Lawton's rancour and his wife's grim expression, I hadn't the nerve.

Matters were not improved by Victoria Helen throwing a tantrum because she didn't want to sit on her grannie's lap. I didn't blame her; used to her other grandmother, Mrs Wardham, and her doting Aunt Helen, she didn't take kindly to this grandmother's exhortations to sit still at the tea-table and not to drop cake crumbs. I'm sure Rose never realised how upset and confused the poor child must have felt when she was removed from her normal surroundings to this small house in Streatham.

Fortunately, Rose's parents departed about six o'clock. Her mother said, 'Although I've locked up everywhere, I don't trust the people in that house. I'm sure that couple on the first floor are no better than they should be, they come in at all hours of the night. I wish we was back in the old street where people were honest and if you liked you could leave your front door unlocked, knowing that none would come in unless invited.'

After the child had gone to bed, Rose produced bottles of port and sherry and we spent a pleasant evening; by common consent her husband was not mentioned. As we left, Rose said, rather wistfully that she'd love to have an evening in the West End with us. Mrs Richard would mind Vicky as Mr Richard 'is away a lot', we chorused.

When I got back, Mr Kite greeted me with the news that Madam had been sorting through her bookshelves and had sent down half-a-dozen books for our servants' hall.

'That's very nice of her, what are they?'

'Well, there's two by Belloc Lowndes – one of them's called *The Lodger*, I think it's about Jack the Ripper. There's two by somebody called Ouida, and the other two are by Arnold Bennett; I like him, he writes about people like us. I've already started on *Riceyman Steps*. Course,' added Mr Kite, slightly maliciously, 'Madam doesn't know that only you and me read proper books.'

Our butler always felt rather peeved that his taste in literature had never influenced Norma, his parlourmaid, to progress beyond *Peg's Paper*. I couldn't see why it was incumbent on him to be a pedant in the pantry. Let everybody be happy in their own way, was my maxim.

My irrepressible kitchenmaid – who should have waited until

the butler was absent – said, 'I like reading books, I'd like to read *The Lodger* if it's about Jack the Ripper. My gran told me about him, she used to live in Whitechapel.'

Mr Kite, irritable as usual when Miriam gave an unasked for opinion, said, sarcastically, 'Is there any incident that occurred in the East End of London when one of your numerous relations wasn't around to record it?'

I hid a smile; it was true that Miriam often related lurid stories of long ago events in London's East End.

Somehow I couldn't see my kitchenmaid remaining in domestic service, she wasn't the type; she'd no idea of respecting the upper servants, of keeping to the rigid hierarchy below stairs. Her mother had told her that life below stairs was lively, that high jinks went on between the servants when they were off duty. Miriam complained that it wasn't like that where we were, it was dull.

'The only kind of place where you would see "high jinks", as you call it,' I said, impatiently, 'is where there is a huge staff that includes several men servants. Not in a place like this where there are only seven living in, and only one of them a male; you can't expect Mr Kite at his age to indulge in high jinks. Miriam, you've no idea what service could be like, this place is the cream. If you had worked under some of the cooks I've had over me, harsh tyrannical slave-drivers, and had to sit at table in the servants' hall with upper servants that demoralised you, then you might have cause to complain. It's because I'm young and remember those days, that I'm easygoing with a kitchenmaid. Why, even when the cook came back from her free evening I'd have to wait on her; take off her shoes, carry hot water along to her bedroom, make her a cup of tea. The only personal chore you do for me is to bring me a cup of tea in the morning. As we have a bathroom, none of you under servants have to bring us hot water. I know that you don't like Mr Kite; but, let me tell you, that in spite of his being prim, prosy and oracular, he's a sight better than some butlers I've known who seemed to imagine that below stairs was a Principality and they the rulers of it.'

Miriam had to listen to this long speech, but I could tell from her expression that none of it really registered. All right, my girl, you just wait, I thought, it won't be long before I leave to get married, you might not be so lucky with the next cook.

Of course domestic service was changing. What with income tax, the cost of living and domestics demanding higher wages, far fewer households could afford to employ a staff of twelve to fifteen. My mother told me that in some of the very large establishments a butler could easily increase his wages by perks. Money on the empty bottles, commission from the shop where he ordered the cigars and, of course, tips from the guests at dinner parties. Mother was a cook in a house where the butler, in addition to the usual perks, had permission to buy necessities for his pantry such as green baize, chamois leathers, rouge and plate-powder for cleaning the silver, and soft cloths for wiping the glasses. As he was never asked to show the bills for these things, quite a bit extra was added.

About two weeks before I finally left domestic service to get married, we three, Rose, Mary and I had an evening in the West End, but it wasn't an unqualified success, mainly because of the absence of the usual reason for going there, to have fun with the opposite sex. Rose had insisted that we do the evening in style, by taking a taxi to Piccadilly and having a dinner at Lyons Corner House there. The food, wine and service were excellent, the band played melodious and romantic airs and, with Rose being so pretty several admiring glances came our way. But we didn't consider ourselves free to take advantage of the 'come-on'; Rose because she was married, I because I very soon would be and Mary because she was faithful to her Conrad. Most of our male conquests were measured by the degree of generosity they showed in buying us chocolates, a decent seat in the cinema and a drink afterwards. But in return for this they expected, and we were prepared to give, a certain amount of petting such as kissing and hugging in dark corners; certainly nothing more than that, though occasionally more was attempted. No doubt the daughters above stairs were not required to give anything in exchange for an evening's entertainment, but then their escorts had not needed to work long and arduous hours to acquire enough money to take a girl out. Still, although three females on their own inevitably lacked the sparkle that male company provided, we enjoyed the evening in our own way. It was the last such evening for me for many years; a milkman's wages allowing only for a beer and a bag of crisps at the local.

Yes, I married. Such a plain and dull statement it seems now, but at the time I was so grateful to get my marriage lines that I nearly framed them. Like a fairy-tale prince who'd roamed the world searching for a bride, only to return to his own home and fall in love with the wood-cutter's daughter – who invariably proved to be a princess in disguise – so did I search for a husband only to find him in the milkman who called every day. I'd assumed he was already married so had not bothered to practise any blandishments on him. Of course he wasn't a prince nor I a princess; but then real life is no fairy-tale.

29

And so I got married and commenced a way of life completely different from the life I'd known since I'd left school at thirteen. It was rather ironical that having just left 'below stairs', our first home happened to be rooms in a basement. In marriage, I tried to put into effect those principles of equality and partnership that to me were the basis of a happy marriage. I thought that the marriage ceremony itself was biased towards the husband with the injunction to 'obey', and the fact that he is not expected to wear a gold ring proclaiming to an army of women searching for husbands, 'I am a married man, hands off'. Having myself a strong antipathy to wearing rings of any kind, I very soon left off wearing a wedding ring. In those days, that was a far greater step forward towards liberty and equality than was – in recent years – the ceasing to wear a bra. A bra-less woman who is wearing a wedding ring is still publicly a married woman, and it's also patently true that over a certain age most women look better wearing a support, whereas not wearing a ring makes no difference to one's appearance. Then I went to free educational classes one afternoon and one evening every week, without my husband; though when the babies arrived I had to give up the afternoon class, my husband not getting in from his milk-round until three o'clock. Later on, when the children went to school, I tried to get up a kind of social and, I was hoping, partly intellectual gathering with some of the mothers, meeting in our own homes; only to discover that most women – working-class wives at least – were as subservient to their husbands' needs as ever we had been to our employers' in domestic service.

Inevitably, I saw much less of Mary and Rose. Mary occasionally came to tea but she preferred, as I would have done, to go as far as Streatham on her free afternoon; not only was it more of an outing, but the food was considerably more sumptuous. With three children in five years, I literally couldn't afford the fare to see Rose. About a year before the outbreak of war, she called on us one evening – we were living in three rooms in Kilburn at that time. She brought Victoria Helen with her and I was surprised to see that now the child was older, she was also prettier. I could sense that Rose was simply bursting with news of some kind, and so it proved. She had, as she put it, that very day set foot in Redlands for the first and only time since she and the son of the house, had departed in the night.

'Oh, Margaret, it was so strange seeing the place after all this time, I thought I'd never have the courage to go up the drive. And what do you think, Mr Hall opened the door. Who'd have thought he'd still be there? And afterwards I went downstairs, and Mrs Buller is still there and Mr Burrows.'

Interrupting this seemingly nonstop flow, I asked the important question: why did she go there?

'Well, Margaret, I had a letter from Vicky's Aunt Helen, to say that Mrs Wardham – I can never get used to saying my mother-in-law – was very ill indeed, and that she'd like to see me and her only grandchild again. And I cried when I saw her, she looked so thin and white and could only whisper, and yet she tried to smile at Vicky. Oh, she was always such a nice lady. And, what do you think, Margaret, Gerald's father was in the hall and he looked as mean and hateful as ever. He wouldn't even look at Vicky and never spoke a word to me. Miss Helen – ' 'your sister-in-law' I interjected – 'said that her father had never spoken to her since she left home, just the same as with Gerald.'

Mary and I seldom mentioned Gerald's name to Rose because she herself never spoke about him. We knew that she still refused to divorce him, but we'd no idea whether or not he was living with his partner's wife. Now suddenly, Rose, perhaps under the stress of revisiting Redlands, said, 'I'm sure that you and Mary think I'm mean and pig-headed because I won't give my husband a divorce. You think what have I got to lose, he'd still support me and Vicky. You don't see it my way. Why should I be an ex-wife? I've done nothing wrong. Why should Vicky, through no fault of hers, or mine, have a divorced father and another woman where her own mother ought to be. Weren't we joined together in holy matrimony in a church? We're legally married not only in the eyes of the law, but we are one in the eyes of the church.'

In all this self-justification I could hear echoes of her mother's sectarianism, her unloving and far from Christian attitude to anybody who strayed from the path of moral rectitude.

Towards the end of the second year of the war my husband was called-up; and then I, with our three sons, left London to live in Hove, my home town. I received an occasional letter from Mary and Rose, which dwindled eventually to a card at Christmas from Mary and nothing at all from Rose, who'd moved down to Devon with her daughter. Then quite suddenly, some months ago, I heard from Mary that Rose had died. It seems incredible to me that so many of that period have gone while I, who nearly died with a massive haemorrhage when I had a gastric ulcer, was knocked down by a car in the middle of the Fulham Road and have had cancer, am still alive and well. I must be, as my sister and I used to say about our mother, indestructible – though I don't really want to live to ninety-four. Even Mary, though only a year or so older than I, has had two heart attacks and lives a very quiet life. Death through old age has taken some of the principal protagonists: the Wardhams, Van Lievdens, Rose's parents and the older servants I knew. Gerald was killed in the last year of the war, and Miss Helen while driving an ambulance. Poor little Vicky, living in Devon to be safe from the air raids, was run over by an army lorry as she ran out of school. Mary never did marry, her Conrad, like his namesake, deciding he preferred to roam the high seas.

When we met again after so many years, there was a great deal of 'do you remember?' We talked of many things; of a life that seems now so remote and alien it is as though it never existed. Like me, Mary is not afraid to talk of death; as she says, it is a journey that one starts upon from the moment of birth. And surely it must be the only journey that the older one gets, the more the speed towards journey's end accelerates? If taken in time, as with mine, doctors can cure some forms of cancer; but for death they can only offer halts on the way. Three years from our golden wedding, my husband and I make jokes that perhaps sound macabre, though to us they are not. Sunday mornings, on the way to our 'local', we pass two cemeteries, the old one on the left, the new on the right. One Sunday he remarked that the new was filling-up rapidly – as is only natural in a town to which old people retire.

'Don't you worry, my love,' I said, 'there'll be room for you. I'll have you buried near to the road so that on the way to the local on my own, I can just throw the flowers over the wall to save me getting out of the taxi.'

'What d'you mean, bury me? I thought we had equality in our marriage?'

'That *is* equality, love. You're five years older than me.' And we laugh and hope we go together.

1. Margaret Powell was an actual kitchen maid and cook in some of the great houses of England, but there have been many *fictional* servants who put their mark on English literature. Which one was your favorite?

2. Margaret chronicles her first lavish dinner party in the Wardham house, a meal with eight courses. Have you ever eaten such a lavish meal and, if so, would you do it again? If you were asked to create a lavish meal today, how many courses would you include and what dish would be the centerpiece?

3. Was the romance of Rose and Gerald like that of Romeo and Juliet or was it different? If so, how?

4. Margaret at once realizes she can't really cook as well as she should when she gets to Kensington. Have you ever been in a position where you were hired for a job that you clearly were not capable of carrying out? If so, what did you do?

5. When Mary and Margaret meet Rose at her new home Melrose, they are on different sides of the servant/master divide. What must this have felt like for them?

6. Has Margaret Powell changed your idea of what servants were like in the era of the great English houses? If so, how?

St. Martin's
Griffin

"*Stands out in the tradition of literature about servants for being a true account . . . although the incidents are as vividly entertaining and disturbing as anything found in fiction.*"

—THE WALL STREET JOURNAL